MASS TORTS
A to Z

Mass Torts A to Z

Legal Industry Experts Reveal Everything Lawyers Need to Know to Start or Grow a Mass Torts Practice

Edward J. Lake, Esq.

Published by Game Changer Publishing

Paperback ISBN: 978-1-7371654-0-8

Digital ISBN: 978-1-7371654-4-6

www.GameChangerPress.com

DEDICATION

This book is dedicated to my parents, Herb and Judi, as well as my wonderful daughters Perri, Risa and Becky.

I would like to acknowledge and thank the authors, all of my employees, clients, vendors and mentors. This book would not be possible without them. A special thanks to Cris Cawley of Game Changer Publishing, Grace Montealegre, the COO of the Persist Group of Companies and Minda Lake...the best ex and best friend any man could hope for.

MASS TORTS A TO Z

Legal Industry Experts Reveal Everything
Lawyers Need to Know to Start or Grow
a Mass Torts Practice

Compilation by Edward J. Lake, Esq.

FOREWORD

I have been asked about writing a book for a while, and since I've been involved in and have been giving advice about the business of mass torts, writing on this subject only seemed natural.

However, as I sat down to collect my thoughts and began to outline (law school skills), I realized that although I know some things about mass torts, except for maybe lead conversion, I am not really an expert in the many areas of mass torts.

Over the last year or so, my team has handled:

- An average of over 200 cases
- An average of 8,000 leads
- Made more than 500,000 calls
- Sent more than 150,000 text messages
- Sent more than 130,000 emails
- Left over 230,000 voicemails

In addition, in my career, my firm has

- Over a billion recovered for our clients by our firm and associated firms
- Worked with over 100 law firms to build their mass tort docket

- Spoken at and attended over 100 legal marketing and management conferences in the past 20 years

So, as you can see, I have had a lot of experience with marketing and lead conversion for law firms.

That is where the idea of a compilation came from. Being in the legal profession for over 25 years and in mass torts almost 20, I have come across many of the actual experts. So, I reached out to some of the best and brightest in the industry for their insights regarding their area of expertise.

Each of the leaders/experts/authors has extensive experience and knowledge in this field and should anyone reading this book like an introduction to any of the experts in this book, please feel free to email me. All of them will gladly help.

As CEO of Leaders in Mass Torts, I hope you enjoy and learn a lot from each of these leaders. They are the best of the best.

Look out for our future podcasts where my team and I will interview the experts of this book and go into further detail regarding their respective areas of expertise.

-EJL

AUTHOR BIO

Edward Lake is one of the founding partners of Gacovino Lake, a personal injury and mass tort firm in operation for over 25 years, located in Long Island, NY. Gacovino Lake's time-tested client follow-up system, training, and procedures are the cornerstones of the firm's success. In 2015, Mr. Lake founded Persist Communications, Corp., based in Fort Lauderdale, Florida. Here he launched a revolutionary system, Persist™ Software, which automates business communications for lead, package, and client follow-up.

When Gacovino Lake first implemented Persist™ Software into their day-to-day procedures, the firm experienced a dramatic change in both conversion and productivity. Because Persist™ runs in the background, the productivity of agents was tripled, and in some cases, even quadrupled.

Persist™ Software enabled Gacovino Lake to increase conversions, decrease their overhead, and reduce the hassles and errors that come with manual call center agent tasks. Agents are no longer expected to leave voicemails, send text messages, manually schedule or send emails, or even make notes for each activity. Instead, Persist™ Software generates notes based on each activity performed. Agents are now able to spend their time doing what they do best—speaking with people.

Persist Communications Corporation makes this software system available to other law firms and businesses across the country, so that businesses can set up their own automated communication sequences. Learn more about Persist™ Software at www.ForPERSIST.com

TABLE OF CONTENTS

PART ONE: - THE CHAPTERS

PART TWO: - THE EXPERT INTERVIEWS

INTRODUCTION

Harlan Schillinger

When I first met Ed Lake some 25 years ago, I simply did not know how to take him and what to do with him. I immediately knew that I was with a unique, interesting and knowledgeable person of great interest.

I listened carefully as Ed laid out his vision of Mass Torts and how to capture business. After a few minutes I realized I was hearing golden words of wisdom that just made sense. That is where it all began for me. Interestingly enough, it began for many of us at that time as well.

From the very early days of Mass Torts and Legal marketing the word Persistence kept coming out of Ed's mouth. He said time and time again in many encounters that followed, "You Have to Be Persistent." Persistence and relentlessness are the backbone of Ed Lake.

Ed Lake taught us many things over the years. With his persistent drive and never-ending energy, I was taught how to make garbage into gold. Lots of gold from what was perceived as dead garbage. He showed us how to take what was labeled dead leads and how to turn them into a pile of qualified and productive cases. Persistence in tracking down every single lead to get a yes or no, is what we are talking about. Ed then went onto generating leads and showing us how to sign-up cases nationally with efficiency, substance and profitability. Still, that unconventional personality was always there. No one is surprised that the Persist Group is the name of Ed Lake's companies.

I believe that Ed's greatest accomplishment and biggest contribution to our industry is his integrity. Integrity is a very broad and bold word. He simply does what he commits to doing, under all circumstances.

Along with his great passion, his family, his zest for travel, finding great wines and his consistent humbleness, Ed is a pretty cool cat.

The pages that follow will help guide you to profits and prosperity. Take what is said and mold the opportunity into your own personality. You cannot lose if you listen.

Respectfully,

Harlan Schillinger

Harlan Schillinger has four decades of experience in legal advertising with a passion for legal marketing, intake and conversion. Harlan has worked with more than 120 law firms in over 98 markets throughout North America. Currently, he is consulting privately only with lawyers who share his vision of increasing business, being accountable and obtaining high-value cases. He takes, perhaps, the most unique and accountable approach to intake and conversion and insists on complete accountability within that arena. In early 2017, Harlan retired from Network Affiliates of Lakewood, Colorado, the nation's first and largest legal advertising agency. He was the leader of their attorney marketing efforts for over 33 years. Prior to joining Network Affiliates in 1985, Harlan was Vice President and one of the founding partners of Madison, Muyskens & Jones advertising agency in Lakeville, Connecticut. In 1975, along with his partners, Harlan founded the first syndication TV production firm for retailers and lawyers, creating television commercials that aired throughout the United States and Canada. Since 1979, Harlan has worked aggressively, productively and professionally within the legal advertising space. When asked about his approach to legal marketing and client relationships, Harlan says, "Creating opportunities and increasing market share for advertising law firms is my #1 priority. The value of the case is everything in such a crowded market." Harlan is an intricate part of the National Trial Lawyers Executive Summit committee as well as a senior editor for the National Trial Lawyers Magazine.

Chapter 1

GETTING THE HIGHEST ROI ON ADVERTISING WITH LEAD CONVERSION

Edward Lake, Esq.

Chief Executive Officer at the Persist Group of Companies

One area that most law firms underperform is lead conversion. Firms spend large sums of money on lead generation, procurement, client services and litigation, but do not put the necessary resources into ensuring firms the best return on investment (ROI) for their advertising dollars by ensuring the best possible conversion of leads.

Many attorneys, who rightfully concentrate on the quality of the legal services they perform, have the attitude that if a potential client does not respond after 1 or 2 attempts at contact, it is easier to just purchase new leads and spend more money on advertising.

But experience has shown me that this is not a good strategy. This leaves too many prospective clients on the table. My philosophy has always been to squeeze the lemon (leads) to get as much juice as possible.

So, how do lawyers get their highest ROI?

Persistence... Persistence... Persistence!

Follow up, follow up, follow up!

The next thing I often hear is, "ok Ed, I agree that I need to do better follow up, so tell me how." There are many ways to follow up with clients, the most effective, even today, is phone calls. That requires more funds for more call center agents. It also means having to deal with staffing issues, not something that most lawyers want.

What I have found after almost 30 years of advertising and lead conversion in the legal field is that not only is technology available to increase ROI, but it is also imperative that law firms know what technology is available in order to reach prospective clients.

I suggest using as many ways of communicating to potential clients as possible. They include:

-texting

-speed dialing with voicemail

-emailING

-chatbot

-video messaging

The reason I suggest using **ALL** the above methods of contact is simple... no one knows which one is best for any potential client.

Normally this requires a lot of work by a lot of staff and if it is not done in a logical sequence it can seem disjointed and unprofessional. To address this problem in my own law firm I developed Persist™ Software platform which attempts to make contact using all the forms of contact listed above. And it does it in a methodical, logical way. You can see what I mean by going to forPERSIST.com and clicking on the video provided.

Whether you decide to use Persist™ or something similar, I encourage you to do so. You will likely see an increase in conversions of a minimum of 15%. Costs of follow-up and call center agents will decrease (no more manual calls, texts, or emails), and your clients will have a better experience.

And I can say that being proactive in educating myself about technology and implementing as much as possible, it has not only increased our internal ROI and improved client and internal staff communications, it has given me a competitive advantage over those who are slow to embrace technology as an integral part of their law firm.

Technology for lawyers is no longer the future. It is the present. Every law firm must know what technology is available to make them more profitable, better communicators, and maximize their clients' experience.

Look out for the next book, *Tech for Law Firms,* in the next few months.

Edward Lake, Esq. is an experienced personal injury attorney and founding partner of Gacovino Lake – a personal injury law firm headquartered in Long Island, New York. Ed has put his innovative and creative marketing skills to work in the area of mass torts to help build some of the biggest inventories of personal injury, medical malpractice, and mass tort cases throughout the U.S. His experience in marketing, lead generation and retainer follow-up, together with associations with the leading plaintiff product liability trial firms in the country, gives him the ability to offer excellent co-counseling options and marketing for lawyers while serving the clients' best interests. Ed is also CEO and founder of Persist Communications and the primary developer of Persist™, a software program which automates communications between businesses and their prospects/clients/customers as well as the CEO of Leaders In Mass Torts (www.LeadersInMassTorts.com), a legal marketing company.

Chapter 2

PAY PER CALL

Adam Warren

CEO of OpenJar Concepts and The Sentinel Group

When it comes to case acquisition, *Performance Media* wins the day. However, like anything else, there are pros and cons. Defining performance, think about it as contingent media. You only pay for the media when it successfully drives to a prospective client or lead. The cost of that lead is how results are quantified and cases are obtained. Therefore, you may have a case that costs $100 per lead or call of typically thirty seconds or greater. If you have a cost per case goal of $500, then we would need at least one in five calls to convert. This is a fairly simple yet highly effective formula for campaign management. Most campaigns convert at one in four to five as a conservative average. That being said, no two cases are alike so if you are buying Roundup and 3M, you should not expect the same cost per case or lead.

There are few platforms or strategies other than attorney referrals and co-counsel agreements that can compete with pay per action. Not even COVID-19 can stop it. These are strategies that have withstood all market factors prior to Covid-19 and continues to do so. In fact, as audiences fragment (especially in these times), law firms should consider this technique as a way to insulate themselves from some risk and use the current environment to their advantage. When law firms began struggling on single event cases back in March of 2020 due to the quarantines, there was a noticeable market shift to reaching potential plaintiffs through a mass-market reach platform than earlier in the year. While there are other formattable strategies in media, such as Cash Buying, which we can deploy at any moment, there are limitations to which performance does not typically endure. For example, when using a pay-per-call or lead strategy, the amount of inventory that any particular campaign can reach would be impossible to mimic with media buying. There would be so many networks, stations and clearances to track as well as purchase, one agency would not be able to manage that. Additionally, while media buying allows for specific day parts and program targeting, you are still paying for every single spot no matter what the outcome is. That is not the case with performance. It sounds hard to believe but it does not matter if one hundred spots clear on a network, if nobody calls or goes to a landing page to submit a form fill, nothing is paid. Acquiring media for pennies on the dollar when dealing with a rigid cost per case allowable is very attractive to firms now and gives them a way to align costs and investment in real-time.

Throughout the years, performance has been a proven strategy that time and time again is called upon for helping law firms find cases using TV, Radio and Print. Today and more so than ever, digital strategies such as social media marketing and landing pages have taken an important seat at the performance table, driving acquisitions up and costs down. All forms of media, if managed properly and transparently, have been able to form a cohesion within a very important and required distinction between a price per call or lead and a cost per case acquired.

Why is this all relevant? As this is written, the world is in the grasp of a global pandemic, yet case acquisition moves forward. One reason, drug and medical device cases do not have borders. The very nature of mass tort marketing is national and therefore your firm's own potential plaintiff pool increases astronomically in comparison to one's own single market where you are typically speaking with tens and tens of people a week hoping for that percentage of rejections to finally kick in a monster single event case. Imagine growing that to hundreds of touch points per day from around the country, seven days per week. Additionally, there are several qualified and proven intake facilities that you can source to relieve pressure internally on your firm's intake staff. This means you can still focus on your single event practice at the same time. Another important reason is most campaigns in tort are an aggregate of law firms coming in to find cases. It goes without saying some firms will have greater means to invest than others which is why this type of marketing is so beneficial to law firms. The aggregation of leads, while all leads and cases are exclusive, allows for small, medium and large firms to come together to create large and inclusive campaigns. There are plenty of instances where these campaigns are exclusive as well, which comes down to a given firm's ability to carry it and take all that comes with it.

What should you look for when seeking a performance media partner for your case acquisition? Starting with the obvious, reputation and longevity. If the company you are looking to engage has tenure and consistent participation in campaigns, they probably have a track record of delivery and integrity. Your partner should have technology that allows for clear view into calls coming in, caller identifiers such as city, state, zip, call durations, listen features and spend to name a few. The ability to integrate with in-house software or third-party legal intake facilities is of paramount importance. We use our proprietary system called TrafTrack®, which has become a feature clients depend on for real-time updates as they need it. Everyone in the given campaign should be reading from the same sheet of music. Finally, reach is key. A one-trick pony using a single form of media is not going to cut it for this ride. Media platforms should be diverse or agnostic to translate the case economics to any platform from TV, Print, Radio and Digital.

Some parting words of advice relate to the creative used to represent your firm. In the current landscape, firms need to stand out. Law firms should look to be innovative both in operations and how the firm is presented to the public. The first place to look is the use of creativity in advertisements. When Covid-19 struck and our live-action production plans were paused, we enhanced our law firm branding efforts using pre-existing footage, higher value motion stock footage, fresh voice offer and innovated new motion graphics unique to each commercial. These effects are eye-popping and increase the likelihood of being noticed.

Adam Warren has worked in entertainment or advertising since producing his first feature film in 1997 and publishing his first children's book in 2017. He and his family reside in Temecula, CA which also happens to be home to OJC and our legal marketing brand and division, TSG. After a respectable run as a creative, advertising sales became his calling. Starting as a sales rep for the national TV advertising firm TeleRep, Los Angeles to heading up media for a performance firm for five years prior to forming OJC, Warren was able to learn the ins and outs of media from local TV stations, local cable, syndication and national network cable. Over time, his knowledge base expanded to radio, print and now the highly sought-after digital landscape. In 2009, upon joining forces with partner Reno Renaldo at the peak of the recession, OpenJar Concepts ("OJC") was born. The core mission then and now is finding quality media that backs into an acquisition cost amenable to media and clients. One year later in 2010, The Sentinel Group ("TSG") entered the equation as the legal focus and primary legal marketing brand of OJC. TSG has remained as a brand on air in various forms of media for fifty-two weeks per year every year, playing a pivotal role in the acquisition of nearly every national campaign for medical devices and medications that caused endless pain, suffering or death. If it is TSG or another trusted partner, pay per call or pay per lead can change your game. The first thing you need to do is identify a campaign and try it.

Chapter 3

FINANCING

Bill Tilley

President & CEO of Amicus Capital Group

As an industry veteran who has been financing and managing contingent-fee law firms and their advertising campaigns across the country for the better part of 25 years, I have witnessed and successfully navigated several market disruptions, with the largest two being the financial crisis a little over a decade ago and the current Covid-19 pandemic that is eclipsing all in size and duration.

We have always focused on working with great trial lawyers that are also great business operators, emphasizing efficiency in the law firm space as profit margins have been tightening for many years. This focus has been vital and allowed us to thrive during these significant market disruptions. Legal advertising pre-COVID-19 had already become hyper-competitive in both the personal injury and the mass tort space and the pandemic has only accelerated this further. We expect this to give a further advantage to those who can advertise and retain cases efficiently and at scale.

Great lawyering with scale and efficiency has thrived and gained market share during every market disruption to date and is even more true today. I am optimistic for the future and expect the market to improve steadily as this pandemic will force even more firms to focus on the effectiveness of their campaigns as well as their overall operations. That being said, there certainly are challenges that must be addressed to succeed in coming out of this crisis.

One such major headwind during this past year has been all of the court closures; while the extent and time of closure have varied state by state, it has been significant. By the second half of 2020, we started to see court closures impact cash flow as settlements slowed due to vacated trial dates. This certainly has eased later in 2020 as some states began to open up and became more efficient with utilizing Zoom-like video options for hearings and even some trials.

A significant difference during this crisis, which has been a net positive, is the massive influx of government aid into the legal market that didn't happen during the 2008 financial crisis. It is estimated that roughly $12 billion was injected into the legal space through PPP and various Economic Injury loans. This has shored up law firms balance sheets across the country and has allowed the excellent operators to invest in new practice areas and launch new advertising campaigns.

When the entire country started shutting down in March and April, there was a tremendous reduction in automobile accidents with so many cars removed from the road. This led to many firms pausing or just outright terminating their advertising campaigns, as no one knew when things would restart. With regard to advertising campaigns, and specifically with personal injury campaigns, we have seen a significant increase in the cost to acquire a new case due to the shrinking pool of potential claims.

As states started to open and people have slowly increased their activity levels, there has been a corresponding increase in case volumes, though they are still significantly lower than pre-pandemic.

We expect this new normal of a reduced case pool in the personal injury space to continue through this year and beyond, forcing more firms to look for new growth opportunities in new practice areas.

As previously stated, firms operating with scale and efficiency were already at a significant advantage when it came to advertising and acquiring new cases. Due to this need, we expect to see more mega and multi-state firms created either through rapid and intentional organic growth, acquisition of market competitors, or via multi-firm collaborations. This trend started pre-pandemic and has since been turbo-charged.

As you continue to see per case profitability reduced due to current market conditions through traditional methods of acquiring cases, you will likely see more conventional personal injury firms ad additional practice areas such as mass torts or hourly practices in order to increase revenue and improve cash flow.

Lawyers need to focus on their operation's key metrics and any area outside of their core expertise. They need to bring in outside talent or hire someone who is an absolute expert. Our industry is mature and there are many great mentors and partners with specific expertise available. Whether you need guidance with operations, hiring, financial leverage, or advertising campaigns, the expertise is available, so go and acquire it.

The overall theme would undoubtedly be that great lawyers are essential and must leverage their talent through scalable and efficient operations that utilize as much automation as available. I am more optimistic than ever about the legal marketplace as we continue to expand our presence. I believe that the market will continue to reward terrific trial lawyers who attract and retain talented partners.

Bill Tilley is a visionary in the ever-evolving field of Litigation Finance and Law Firm Management. Bill is more than just an entrepreneur; he is a leader in law firm growth and risk mitigation. As the Litigation Finance Industry Pioneer and having funded, facilitated, and managed north of a billion in transactions and budgets, no one has a more in-depth knowledge of the complete metrics of running a law firm. Through the Amicus Group of companies, Bill continues to transform the business of law.

Chapter 4

MINING YOUR CURRENT CLIENT DATABASE FOR GOLD

Grace Montealegre

COO for the Persist Group of Companies

There is a quote by Jack Kerouac in *On the Road* that captures my feelings about business. "[...] the only people for me are the mad ones, the ones who are mad to live, mad to talk, mad to be saved, desirous of everything at the same time, the ones who never yawn or say a commonplace thing, but burn, burn, burn like fabulous yellow roman candles exploding [...] across the stars..."

As a marketing professional in different industries (both B2C and B2B) from retail to legal for over twenty years, I have always felt that you must be a little "mad" to be successful at business. The urge (desire) to be better to serve your clients in the best way possible is imperative.

There are many statistics that show acquiring a new client is always going to be more expensive than "re-acquiring" a current client. Besides the obvious reasons, i.e., current clients already know, like and trust your company; there are other far-reaching and as important reasons why a current client would be more inclined to "purchase" from you versus another company. COVID has made this connection to current clients even more important. Nearly all companies were forced to become fully remote. There are many pop-up companies selling their wares online than ever before, creating a unique opportunity for those firms that already send client or prospect communications to remind their clients that they are there to help. This is the time to ramp up that outreach. Why is now the time?

COVID has made individuals even more leery of online companies and has shifted the way people buy and why. This behavior is called consumer behavior. Consumer behavior is the study of people and how they make purchase decisions to satisfy their needs, wants or desires, and how their emotions play into the decision to buy. It is mainly concerned with psychology, motivations, and behavior – why a person buys something. Coupled with life cycle marketing, marketing based on where a prospect or current client is in the "sales funnel," a law firm can be successful in pulling the most out of their current list.

Many law firms and other businesses have created avatars, user journeys or other ways to identify purchasing behavior for prospects or clients and where the prospects and clients are in the funnel (aka life cycle). As an example, a current client who is in the litigation process should get a different set of communications than a prospect who has never been a client versus one who has already had a disbursement or case settled. Communications of any kind must be personalized to the individual, including where they are in the life cycle of their interaction with your firm to be effective.

Since the power of information is in the hands of the consumer, they require many more touchpoints to get through the typical "sales" funnel to make that decision to buy from your company. Therefore, you must, as a business, stay top-of-mind with all current clients and prospects. The power is still in the list, but not if you do not use it or "mine it for gold." But how?

This is where marketing automation and communication technology lend a hand. Implement automation including, but not limited to, calling, voicemail drops, emailing, texting and chatbots. Place all prospects or current clients in a nurture funnel. This is information distributed to your contacts (client or prospective client) in a personalized funnel sent in the method and/or methods the individual prefers. As an example, let us say a current client in your list had a personal injury case with your firm. Your firm could place them into a nurture campaign (funnel) that keeps your firm top-of-mind and lets them know what other practice areas or injuries you handle. You could send voicemail drops, emails or other non-intrusive communications to the client, letting them know what else you offer. Your firm needs to take this opportunity to also make the ask. What is "the ask"? This is the call to action. Make sure to determine your goal and objective prior to creating a nurture campaign and then create the funnel as appropriate to the stage of the client in your life cycle and always make the ask. Any communication to a client or prospect in a funnel must have a call to action, "the ask," i.e., it can be as simple as "refer our firm to your loved ones."

Marketing technology does not have to be complicated; it should be an enhancement and complement your current tech tools. As a law firm, look at your current communications and marketing strategy, use what you have and enhance your technology tools with something like Persist™ Software (automates communication by calling, emailing, and texting prospects and clients automatically in a campaign sequence). Whatever you use, start now and mine your current client database for gold!

Grace Montealegre has over fifteen years of experience in marketing on every level. Specializing in marketing automation and technology, she has worked with different industries and in both B2C and B2B markets. From legal marketing to steel to software and communications, Grace has a breadth of knowledge spanning nearly every industry and demographic. Grace is currently the Chief Operations Officer for the Persist Group of Companies, including Persist Communications (www.ForPERSIST.com)

and Leaders in Mass Torts (www.LeadersInMassTorts.com). She has spoken at multiple events as a subject matter expert, most recently at the Intrigue Digital Marketing Summit in Miami on May 8th, 2019. Grace also co-hosts a podcast on legal marketing called InCamera podcast. (www.incamerapodcast.com)

Chapter 5

ETHICS

Chris McDonough Esq.
Special Counsel to the Firm FOLEY GRIFFIN LLP

I have been practicing exclusively in the field of professional ethics for over 30 years. The first 13 years I was a grievance prosecutor for New York State. Those 13 years allowed me to observe the mistakes that many attorneys make and probe as to why they made them. Since 2002 I have defended lawyers facing grievances and counseled lawyers seeking to avoid grievances and market their practices. Involved in the practice of law as I am, I have had the opportunity to see how Covid has impacted the practice and lawyers. I have seen how it has affected my attorney clients as well as our law firm.

In brief, I have seen lawyers scrambling to adjust to a new reality. Some have made changes allowing them to proceed as before. Some have closed their offices and taken employment elsewhere or retired.

This pandemic has been terribly impactful to our society, including lawyers and law firms. Court closures, suspension of jury trials, extended statutes of limitation, virtual appearances, etc., have reduced lawyer retention and income. However, to some firms, this has been a teachable moment whose lessons must be translated into positive changes in their practice.

While the pandemic will eventually come under control, I believe some of the changes it has wrought will remain. Lawyers who do not adapt to these changes may fail.

Some traditional law firm processes, including but not limited to marketing and client retention, may be changed permanently. In my own situation, our firm was shuttered for many months with lawyers working remotely unless absolutely necessary. Now, eight months since the pandemic began, I use the Internet almost exclusively to communicate and work with my clients. Instead of setting aside an hour for an office consultation, I can do multiple consultations via virtual meetings at the same time. This saves a substantial amount of time, especially where it eliminates the need to travel.

Covid has also forced lawyers to develop systems and procedures for working remotely and for effective intra-firm cooperation and communication. Many lawyers I speak to have come to realize that with these new processes in place they have experienced increased productivity, allowing them to operate with reduced staff and lower overhead, thus increasing profit.

Marketing has also been greatly impacted. In-person round tables, public presentations, lunches, etc., have been replaced by list serves, chat rooms, and interactive websites. A firm's "face" no longer is a palatial space with cherry wood walls. Its website will now be how a firm makes its impression upon potential clients. Your website must be professional and interesting. Clients are sophisticated and will react negatively to a poor website, the same as if a lawyer greets a client at the office in a stained and rumpled suit.

I believe that the implementation and reliance upon the use of systems for operating a law firm and the increased dependence upon internet marketing will remain. The pandemic has taught us that a leaner firm that focuses upon using its staff more effectively will increase profit.

Focusing upon Internet marketing, rather than traditional advertising, is essential. While these trends have been coming for a few years now, this pandemic has pushed them to the forefront.

Moving forward, lawyers must keep the lessons learned from Covid in mind. Remote working and virtual client interaction and court appearances save firms enormous amounts of time. But to do so effectively, you must have systems in place that all employees understand and that are enforced. A reliable software system and high-quality cameras and computers will allow you to present your firm in a more professional light.

If you are now more heavily reliant upon virtual practice, you likely will find that you don't need as much office space as you may have in the past. A clean professional-looking office for remote appearances and client conferences is essential. But, if your staff attorneys are mostly working remotely, consider office sharing or other actions to consolidate your space where feasible.

However, avoid the impulse to over-use interactive websites. Careless exchanges of case-specific information can result in a client assuming an attorney-client relationship has been created and can lead to a court upholding that one has been constructively created based upon the client's realistic presumptions. Further, take care relying on outside website administrators. If they are not familiar with the restrictions on lawyer advertising and solicitation, they could inadvertently violate your state Code, for which you will be held accountable.

Finally, don't just jump back into replacing staff that may have been laid off because of Covid. Make sure you truly need that person before committing to their salary, benefits, etc. Being a terrible typist, I have been dictating my work. What I now present to my assistant for formatting and sending out is a much more polished product than in the past, thus reducing her workload. As the other lawyers in our firm also do this, we have been able to operate fully on our reduced staff.

Change is inevitable. Whether change is forced upon us or is a conscious choice, you must adapt to the new reality and, where possible, take advantage of it or be left behind.

Chris McDonough is an attorney who has spent his 30 plus year legal career practicing and educating exclusively in the field of professional ethics. He has taught ethics as an Adjunct Professor and regularly presents CLE courses for bar associations, attorney associations, firms, etc. He has authored numerous articles for texts, law reviews, the New York Law Journal, and other publications. He has been certified as an expert on professional ethics and the practice of law by various courts throughout New York State. He can be reached via Newyorkethicslawyer.com or FoleyGriffin.com.

Chapter 6

FUNDING A MASS TORT PRACTICE

Jeff Huff

President of American Law Firm Capital

With the introduction of COVID-19 into the world we are certainly in unprecedented times. It seems undeniable it will change the way how all businesses including Law Firms operate in 2020 and beyond. Over the past 20 years our team at American Law Firm Capital has been fortunate to work with thousands of plaintiff law firms and hundreds of mass tort lawyers. This lending experience while we were also executing during two of the last three financial crises serves as the basis of this article.

Our goal is to help you with the new and related "Business of Law" practices in order to assist you THRIVE not just survive during these new times.

First, we'll quickly review past financial crashes, lessons learned and what we believe that you can expect from our current COVID- Crash. We'll then move into suggestions and actionable items to help you better acquire loans for your firm while increasing profits.

The Past 3 Financial Crashes

Over the past 33 years, we've had three major stock market crashes: 1987, the Dot.com Bust (2000 through 2003) and the Financial Meltdown (2007 through 2008). There have also been at least an equal number of mini crashes in between, with the most recent occurring in the last quarter of 2018

The more immediate relevance of the past three crashes is the last bear market in U.S. stocks which occurred between October 2007 and March 2009. During that time, the S&P 500 plummeted nearly 57%. The recent Coronavirus Crash reached 35% between February and March of 2020 and the repercussions are still bubbling.

What lessons have we learned, and as a result, what can you expect from this newest crash?

Tighter Credit Criteria for Law Firms: Similar to the 2008 housing crash, COVID-19 will have a significant and most likely a much greater impact on the U.S. economy than the 2008 crisis. In fact, many at Wallstreet are expecting the financial impact of the COVID Crash to exceed the 2000 Dot.com and the 2007 Financial Mortgage crisis combined. As a result, expect the amount of due diligence on your firm to increase from your bank or other alternative capital resources, underwriting methodologies will vary depending on the lender and the requirements they have from their capital partners. Whether the capital sources to those entities are the Federal Government, accredited investors, family offices or hedge funds, your firm will be under much higher scrutiny and Lender's due diligence will get much more granular. As a result, fewer loans will be made to law firms and only to those able to show strong character along with solid collateral and business practices.

Availability of Capital – You can expect that once the U.S. Government's financial stimulus to small businesses has ceased, capital resources will be much more limited as various sources of capital have taken significant hits on liquidity and their balance sheets. Capital will be looking to take less risk and again be more particular to whom they lend.

Timelines to Fund – As a result of increased funding criteria, availability of capital and lower risk tolerance, expect funding timelines for you to acquire capital will be lengthened.

Rates – With zero percent interest rates should go down, right? Unfortunately, not for lumpy cash flowing law firms whose assets generally don't meet Federal Banking guidelines, expect rates to go up. As of April of 2020, industry rates have already risen as risk has increased substantially. As a result of more fragile balance sheets and unpredictable sustainability of many law firms and defendants, capital will build in additional loss factors. Rates will vary significantly depending on your portfolio type, diversification, the leverage on your firm, your historical track record, business acumen and stability.

OK, considering the lessons and reality of all the above, how does your firm prepare for the new post COVID business environment?

Although he was referencing Isolation in space versus our current isolation at home due to COVID-19, I believe Mark Kelly, an Arizona Astronaut, said it well, "This is the new reality, put a plan in place." As a proponent of business plans, we find it very troubling that only 33% of most companies have a written business plan. **Statistics show that those with a plan get a loan or investment capital 2x that of a company without a plan and growth of the company with a plan is typically 50% greater.**

Key Loan Attributes – Getting Your Plan in Order

Character & Disclosure – The first attribute most lenders look at is the personal character of the firm partners, not your collateral (cases) or your balance sheet. While lenders are sympathetic to the target on your back regarding bar complaints, litigation and other claims against you, your personal character is a major indicator to the lender of your stability, ability to perform and protect the collateral they have secured. Things happen in life and business. When they do their best to provide full disclosure of any past issues, be prepared with written explanations and supporting documentation for your lender. Most character issues can be explained and overcome. However, non-disclosure may be the kiss of death.

Human Capital – This crisis has unconditionally expedited how and where employees will work from. It was already predicted that 50% of future employees would work remotely by 2030 and/or be consultants versus employees. It appears 2030 is here now. Now more than ever it will be important to have well-defined employment or consulting agreements. As your team works remotely, your expectations and their accountability will change, be critical to your success and servicing your clients. Now is the time to also invest in companies that can provide and identify specific personality profile attributes for your employees or consultant candidates who can execute in this new remote business model. Surrounding yourself with a group of like-minded leaders with attributes in alignment with your new 2030 model will be key in your human capital resources and new hires.

Corporate Documents – Have these documents readily available. They include your articles of incorporation, state certificate of good standing, bar status, operating agreements or bylaws showing ownership and authority, buy-sell agreements, succession plans, employee manuals, partner vesting schedules and bonus programs, all insurance products and any real estate owned by the firm.

Affiliated Companies, Past or Other Firm's you own – Fully disclose and have clearly defined agreements between all current and past entities you own and/or make payments between. Lenders are fearful of claw-backs, non-market agreements, or diversion of income to any entity you may currently or have owned in the past. Expect loan covenants or disclosures regarding all your entities.

Commingling – Never commingle bank accounts or other company assets that could jeopardize your corporate veil, confuse and concern your lender. If employees or other operational costs are shared, again have clear written agreements, inter-company loan documents, or fee share agreements in place. If you have multiple firms using the same case management systems have clearly defined sub-folders or, better yet, different versions to eliminate confusion of who owns the portfolio of cases.

Co-Counsel Agreements – Have signed, ethically opined agreements in place with all outside co-counsel clearly defining fee shares, expenses and other key criteria agreed upon. A handshake or short email between firms is almost always inadequate and discouraged. Lenders can't loan you money if they can't clearly define what assets you own. Also, depending on your state, this is also a good time to visit your client retainers and address the pass-through of interest to your clients.

Financial Statements & Tax Returns – Lenders understand the poor financial model plaintiff lawyers have inherited. We use much of your historical financial information to predict cash flow and your ability to repay a loan. They're also a good indicator of your integrity and business acumen. Be prepared to provide the last two years of your most recent tax returns, three years of your internal financials, including the most recent quarter of any year and the personal financial statements of each firm owner with more than 10% equity. Disclose all outstanding liens and loans, providing your track record of past loan performance can also be very beneficial. If you have engaged a consultant or broker, disclose their written agreement, including all fees negotiated.

Budget & Cash Flow –In addition to the previous items addressed, understanding, preparing and monitoring cash flow is absolutely one of the most important functions you, your CFO or accountant perform. This exercise will help provide a roadmap to execute and give you a solid understanding of your long-term capital needs. It will also keep you disciplined in spending, especially when you receive those larger settlements you worked so hard to obtain. Look at your last few years of historical expense information, and also predict any other future additional or non-recurring expenses, whether it's the acquisition of a new key employee like a CFO, new capital expenditures, PSC fees or others. After assembling your budget and use of funding proceeds, be realistic about your case values and settlement timelines. The combination of revenue timing and expenses over the next several years will determine your cash flow needs and ability to repay your loan. And of course, always be good stewards of money.

Collateral & Clean Data – In addition to many other functions, accurate and clean data from your case management system reflects the basis of your firm's portfolio or collateral value. Vendors and your staff all interface at different times and affect different data points. Training of employees and carefully choosing vendors throughout the entire life cycle of a case is something that needs close attention. Vendors that can provide their specific services and integrate them with other vendors while providing and orchestrating training to your staff is ideal. Members of the Mass Tort Vendor Association are good resources to help you. Basic data points to acquire include a unique client ID affiliated with, but as a separate identifier to protected HIPAA data. In addition, you should be continually tracking the "worked up" status on each of your client's cases throughout the entire lifecycle of their case. These data points should include but not limited to the current legal status, all qualifying injuries and/or specific qualifying criteria including any medical exclusions and legal items or milestones such as but not limited to SOL and pending trial decisions. Make sure your employees are entering accurate data and using consistent, precise language in the data entry process. Your Lender will need these clean data points to confirm your cases are viable and to help them determine the total borrowing base value of your portfolio, all of which tie back into your cash flow product that determines the loan amount you qualify for and your ongoing borrowing needs. I will save the topic of technology that Segway's into the above for those experts.

Finally, It's time for you to brag!

Personal & Firm Track Record – Show the Lender you can be a partner who can perform. Assemble all awards and accomplishments, show any leadership positions in law, how you give back to your industry and local community. If you have an area of expertise that is material and supports your portfolio, assembling your past track record, it gives your Lender confidence in your ability to execute.

While we could certainly add topic items and further drill down in many of the above topics, your ability to execute the above Business of Law items orchestrated and in alignment with the Practice of Law will make you a much more viable candidate and could be the difference in your ability to acquire loan proceeds for your firm to assist with the clients and your team that you lead.

As a business owner and entrepreneur for over forty years, these practices have served me well. I'm sure they will do the same for you and our team wishes you success in your continued pursuit of justice.

Jeff Huff is currently President of American Law Firm Capital, LLC; U.S. Law Firm Funding Administration, LLC and the current President of the Mass Torts Vendors Association. Over the past 18 years, Jeff Huff founded four separate finance companies, pioneered & assisted in the development of the U.S. Legal Funding industry by creating a sophisticated, proprietary underwriting methodology for law firms & plaintiffs. He currently leads an experienced team of executives, underwriters, analysts, lawyers & and administrative staff located in New York, Arizona, Florida & California. Beginning in 2010, Jeff began scaling his law firm funding model nationally by servicing the leading Mass Tort firms & providing capital to those firms for operations & portfolio expansion. In 2013 & after his company worked with approximately four hundred mass tort lawyers, his company American Legal Funding, LLC was named one of the "Top Pick" U.S. law firm funding companies in the MDL- Mass Tort litigation niche. That led to the expansion & creation of

American Legal Financial Services, LLC, American Law Firm Funding, LLC & American Law Firm Capital, LLC. Jeff has been an entrepreneur since 1978, sold two prior companies, one of which was scaled to the largest in the United States in its niche with International sales & distribution. Jeff has served on numerous public & private boards, as well as been active in several charities.

Chapter 7

CALL CENTER OUTSOURCE IN U.S.

Scott Fuentes

Partner & Chief Business Development Officer
at Legal Conversion Center

H aving a call center that works with more than 300 law firms and over two dozen advertising firms gave us tremendous insight into the impact of the pandemic on the legal industry. Prior to the pandemic, the economy was stable and single-event cases were coming in steadily. In the tort world, we just finished wrapping up a series of large mass tort campaigns, including Opioids and Boy Scout Abuse. Then the pandemic hit. Some firms struggled to adjust while others flourished. Ultimately many firms needed to outsource their calls to a center like ours and for good reason.

When the pandemic hit and the lockdown orders in many states were enacted, this dramatically affected some firms. First, they were not prepared from an infrastructure standpoint to have employees work from home. Their phone systems, computer systems, and case management systems were not set up to have employees work remotely. Second, many firms did not know how to monitor employees working from home.

Measuring employee productivity was exceedingly difficult. Many firms reached out to our call center to help. Our systems and processes were already set up. Our technology allowed us to seamlessly allow agents to work from home. Our proprietary software allowed us to handle a firm's calls and follow up on new client inquiries, while simultaneously integrating into their firm's case management software. Employee productivity was not an issue because the firms were covered by our services 24/7 and they were only paying for the actual work being done and nothing in between. Although some firms stopped advertising and decided to wait out the storm, other firms adjusted and used our services to help stay afloat.

Some firms took advantage of opportunities during the pandemic. With fewer firms advertising some found an avenue to grow the firm's brand. This was a great opportunity for some firms to get in front of the consumer with less competition for ad space. In addition, successful firms adapted and started to invest in other practice areas, particularly in the mass tort area. Since there was a sharp decline in the number of single-event cases due to the lockdown, there were plenty of resources to expand the firm's client base in other areas. We saw many firms increase their spend on older torts like Zantac, RoundUp, Clergy Abuse, and the newer Texas Power Outage. Our call center services were of great value to these firms. For firms that were just getting into mass torts, they found a reliable and well-informed partner in LCC. We were able to guide these firms in the right direction and get them going with full retainer services, intakes, media partners, and 24/7 coverage. For firms that were already involved in mass torts, we were able to quickly adjust to their increased marketing spend on torts.

Now that we have a vaccine and we are starting to see the country reopen for business, firms are starting to bring employees back, single event cases are on the rise and things are seemingly getting back to normal.

My advice to firms now and in the future is to always be technologically prepared and to diversify their client portfolios. Being technologically prepared means having your infrastructure set up in a way that your phone systems, computer systems, and case management systems are cloud-based and able to accommodate employees working from home. I would also suggest that firms develop an employee productivity standard that can be measured hourly in daily reports. If that seems like a lot of work, then you should look at a service like ours. Firms should also diversify their client portfolio. If you're a PI firm, you should look at adding one or two mass torts to your client base. This will open new revenue streams and allow you to continue advertising and to continue building your brand, even in the toughest of times.

Scott Fuentes is Partner and Chief Business Development Officer at Legal Conversion Center. Scott has more than 12 years of call center experience. He helped build one of the largest legal-specific call centers in the country. Scott is also key in developing many of the industry's leading intake and conversion software for call centers.

Chapter 8

LAW FIRM BRANDING

Donna DeVita

Principal of ESQuire Brand Management

Branding for a law firm is much more than the name of the firm and the logo it represents. *"Brand is everything, and everything is brand,"* this quote is taken from the *Harvard Business Review*, as it is simple and true. Your law firm brand should represent all elements of your business. From your strategy, communications, and advertising to call-to-action, your people, customer service, facilities and more. A brand should be considered your voice. It should be authentic, authoritative, engaging, impactful and memorable for your clients and potential clients to not only trust your brand, but to build brand loyalty for future clients. Let's face it, the majority of people that personal injury law firms market to, are not injured and do not need an attorney. Staying in front of potential clients is essential and how your brand is perceived is key to generating a future case.

During the current pandemic, law firms face new challenges generating new cases. Many firms may believe their branding is strong, especially firms that heavily market and advertise. Yet other firms are now looking at building their brand to survive this uncertain time. Whether you fit within the first or the latter, you should ask yourself these questions regarding your law firm's brand; "How is the firm's brand perceived by our staff, clients and the community we serve?" And "Does our branding represent the firm as strong community leaders that care, advocate and do right?"

The current pandemic has most law firms evaluating every aspect of their business which includes their sources of generating new cases. In the earlier months, during the first "shutdown" phase, we found many law firms scaled back their advertising and digital campaigns and refrained from all forms of new marketing. The reasoning for this varied from budget cuts, status of an uncertain market, to the transitioning of their law firm to operate remotely. However, other clients took advantage of the lower costs in advertising and wider opportunities that opened up when their competitors pulled back. Regardless of the level of advertising during this time, the one consistent and key branding strategy was and continues to be the management of strong firm communications. Firms that are providing ongoing, open, clear information to staff, clients and the community during the crisis, are actively branding with every email, web notification, social media post, webinar, news alerts and more. By using communication tools and positioning the firm as a resourceful leader, during a time of crisis is not only a perfect way to brand your firm without advertising, it's key to keeping your brand one step ahead of your competition.

Many personal injury law firms struggle with the stereotype reputation of being labeled "ambulance chasers." A stigma that has led many law firms to depend only on generating cases from "word of mouth" with the fear of being grouped into the typical hard-hitting firms that advertise "HURT? CALL..." Although this may not be the style of your firm, completely depending on word of mouth without any branding strategies to market the firm, could fall short. Nationally, as the personal injury law firm sector grows and becomes more saturated, law firms cannot ignore the need for branding to help generate new cases.

Another huge branding opportunity for law firms, especially during this pandemic is being visible and present within the community you serve by actively giving back. This does not mean writing a check to charities and donating funds. This means rolling up your sleeves and being seen to help make a difference. Effectively branding the firm via a community outreach program must have the firm's commitment and support. It should not be implemented solely for marketing purposes, to tell a story and "look good." It needs to be part of your firm's culture, representing the firm's story of "doing good."

We have been implementing community outreach initiatives for law firms, throughout the country, for many years. Community outreach events are a perfect opportunity to highly-brand your firm, build brand equity and leave a lasting impression. When considering a giving-back initiative, it is important to evaluate the purpose, message and the expected end result for the firm's support and involvement. There are many charities and causes that need support, but when selecting these it is important that the firm believes in the charity and the cause. Also, as much as we pointed out that giving-back should not be done for the purpose of marketing, it is vital that implementing these types of programs should be supported with strong branding. When there is an opportunity to have the firm present within the community at events, it is important to have those attending these events know who you are and what you do. Marketing your brand is needed for people to make the connection that not just any law firm, but YOUR law firm is doing good. This is effectively done by displaying branded pop-up tents, tables and booths. Wearing logo attire at the events, engaging with branded activities and giving branded promotional items away, known as "swag." Selecting the items to give away should be tailored to the audience of the event while still representing your firm's brand colors, logo and message. Firms that don't put thought into their giveaways can end up with poor-quality branding and items that are less likely to be kept by potential clients.

Although many events have been postponed or canceled during this pandemic, there are still ways to make an impact and brand within the communities you serve. Law firms have been offering their support during this time with implementing food drives to collect food and physically donate to the needy. Buy and serve lunch to essential construction workers, health care providers and other front-line workers. As well as providing branded masks and face coverings or hand sanitizers to existing clients and giveaways via social media campaigns.

It is necessary in today's climate for a law firm to find creative ways to stay in front of their market and build brand recognition. Implementing effective branding strategies will not only help with brand awareness but combined with the right messaging and community outreach it should lead to your brand being known, trusted and favored above your competition.

Donna DeVita, Principal of ESQuire Brand Management, is an award-winning branding & marketing professional with 25+ years experience providing unique branding strategies for her law firm clients. Donna's talent and creativity breathe life into a brand by developing high-impact branding and marketing opportunities that creates brand equity and loyalty. This is proven by her clientele of some of the most successful trial attorneys in the country.

Donna defines herself not just by the successes of her business or clients, but also by her deep commitment to community outreach, mentoring and other charitable works. This is representative of Donna's passion to continuously give back within the communities she lives and serves.

Chapter 9

LAWYER NETWORKING

Seth Price

Founding partner of Price Benowitz LLP & Founder and CEO of BluShark Digital

EXPERTISE:

I was able to take a two-person law firm and scale it to 40 lawyers in less than ten years. One big reason I was able to do this was my ability to network within the industry. I was able to build a large portion of my firm through establishing a solid referral network to maintain a steady stream of cases. I did this mostly through in-person meetings, either over a cup of coffee, at breakfast, or sitting down to lunch.

I'm also a big proponent of attending as many industry conferences as possible. I am often a lecturer and/or moderator at some of the largest law conferences in the United States. These conferences allow you to mingle with others who are likely facing similar obstacles that you may be facing in trying to grow your business, and offer you an opportunity to share ideas about how to overcome those obstacles. They also provide a chance to learn about tools and strategies that can be used to align your business development with changing consumer habits.

One aspect of consumer habits that is not changing, however, and that should be at the forefront of your thinking in terms of how, when, and where to advertise, whether prior to COVID or now, is that you want your firm to stay top-of-mind for both old clients and potential new clients. This can be done by sending regular newsletters and informational touchpoints to your database. You never know when someone may need your services, so being in the right place at the right time could be as simple as making sure to touch your database at least once a month.

PROS AND CONS:

Networking within the industry is essential to continuing to grow your business, and that hasn't changed with the onset of COVID. What has changed are the mediums for doing this. As I mentioned above I'm an in-person meeting kind of guy when it comes to networking, so naturally COVID really put a damper on that type of networking, especially in the first couple months of quarantine. However, I was able to adjust and I found ways to maintain relationship building while still social distancing. I did this through setting up virtual lunches via zoom, offering social distance coffee dates where I allowed the other party to choose the meeting space, and tapping into my local network to find local business owners who were open to allowing me to use their outdoor space to hold meetings.

I project that these types of social distancing networking tactics will need to continue for some time, but even after COVID is over and people feel safe going back to conferences and in-person meetings the strategies for having to figure out how to maintain relationship building while distant can persist. It goes back to what I was saying about staying top-of-mind, and if you're able to do that regularly even if you're in a different city or time zone then chances are those relationships will prevail.

HOW ARE THINGS CHANGING:

There are certain platforms and businesses that have skyrocketed in popularity because of COVID, such as Zoom, Amazon, Facebook, Instagram, Uber Eats, DoorDash and Grubhub. The industry has changed by taking advantage of platforms such as these, and so best learning how to use these types of platforms to your advantage, whether it's for advertising your business or networking with fellow industry professionals, is how I would recommend pivoting if you haven't already done so.

Personally, I use Zoom to set up virtual meetings for networking, but it could also be used to host a monthly or quarterly webinar to educate potential clients on FAQs. I use food delivery services such as Uber Eats and DoorDash to deliver a meal from a local restaurant to a person I'm meeting with for a virtual lunch. I've learned that if you buy someone a meal, they'll give you a listen, and these are platforms that can help with that.

FUTURE EXPECTATIONS:

Even when it is safe to again venture out and meet with people in person without social distancing, there are technological advances that will have been made during COVID that will entice people to keep using them because of their convenience. So firms will have to shift to accommodate both in-person and virtual for a lot of their events and meetings.

ADVICE MOVING FORWARD:

As a business owner you have knowledge that is powerful and helpful to others, so leverage that knowledge to build your potential client and referral lists. There are many ways to do this both virtually and in person, be it through webinars, newsletters, or networking events, so this core mission should not change no matter what the business or economic climate looks like at the time.

Seth Price, Esq. is a founding partner of Price Benowitz LLP as well as the founder and CEO of BluShark Digital. He earned a B.A. in Economics and International Relations from the University of Pennsylvania and his J.D. from the George Washington University School of Law, where he graduated with honors. Seth began his legal career as an insurance litigator at Swindler & Berlin before assisting in launching USLaw.com. As a founding and managing partner of Price Benowitz, Seth oversees a team of more than 40 attorneys with offices in Maryland, Virginia, and Washington, DC. Seth Lives in Bethesda, MD with his wife, Jodi, and their three children.

Chapter 10

LIEN RESOLUTION

Todd Franklin

CEO and Legal Strategist for MASSIVE

MASSIVE: Medical and Subrogation Specialists currently provide resources to law firms across the country for resolving health insurance liens in an efficient and expedient manner. Our transparent technology provides the unprecedented 24/7 support required throughout a case and after settlement. It is vital in today's environment to continually monitor, track, and categorize payments made by Medicare, Medicaid, ERISA, Hospital, or Private Health Insurance (MMEHP) by staying ahead of the subrogation curve. There are a multitude of steps involved before a lien becomes payable.

Process is more important now than ever; it is easy for subrogation to fall behind. Law firms must continue working to keep on task to maintain continuity. We regularly educate law firms on the subrogation process, help investigate its true cost, and work to review procedures, ask questions and to establish a scorecard of related metrics. A scorecard helps pinpoint the pulse of how implemented efficiencies are working.

Attorneys are encouraged to take advantage of MLS's little cost administrative support services allowing for more time to devote themselves to the provision of legal services and advice. In many cases, it has been reported by attorney customers that MLS has reached a resolution with the mlienholder holder at least two months sooner than the attorney would in similar cases while also increasing the plaintiffs' net settlement proceeds.

Law firms generally lack effective or financially well-healed methods for attaining open lines of communication with Medicare and understanding the timing and information dynamics. For example, all medical providers are required to use specific medical billing codes designating a patient's injury. These codes together are called ICD-9 and ICD-10 and are roughly 68,000 of them. MLS mitigates law firm risk as well as gives flexibility to the amount of time law firm personnel must devote to handling the burden of MMEHP liens. MLS helps law firms by providing a route to follow, including early and continual monitoring of a plaintiff's billing codes; proper code management and review; verification of injury-related coding; application of statutory payment reductions; and serving as a conduit for communication between the attorney's office and the government or insurance office requiring repayment.

Law firms are spread out with many employees working from home, it has become important to have information/work results available as needed. Having access to important metrics is paramount to monitoring the firm's results (including subrogation). Law firms have not had the benefit of an expert like MASSIVE until now, one who is dedicated to educating law firms with proven results. Law firms are taking a long look at how outsourcing lien resolution can work for them. Having been thrust into a work from home model might turn out to be the impetus of change. The workload has grown larger, law firms are looking to lien management and asking how we can help.

Recognizing and being able to respond to risk is important to the contingent practice. Unfortunately, many firms have constraints leaving limited time to chart the nuances of Medicare, ERISA, and other complex subrogation. This leaves you open to undue risk (timing, monetary loss, client relations, etc.), these all too familiar results highlight the need for scrutinizing the timing and charting of efficient workflows.

Risk is quietly buried and as a best practice should be mapped so you can see the issues in your workflow to build in escalation processes. Begin by asking risk-oriented questions to get your analysis started, for example:

1. Does your initial sign-up packet include up to date HIPAA authorizations, requests for health insurance information and health insurance cards?

2. How do you establish early contact with the likes of Medicare, Medicaid, or an ERISA plan?

3. Does the firm handle subrogation individually or is there dedicated staff?

4. What is the goal we want to achieve? Improved timing, better process, increased plaintiff net recovery?

Challenge your firm to establish a list of metrics that help get a pulse on your company. Find 5-10 of the most important pieces of information available that can get you to that pulse.

Once you have begun to identify and isolate these metrics, study how to minimize or even eliminate risk factors. Build step-by-step workflows and have staff follow those efficiencies. Most important is to train your staff to understand the importance of following the workflow, and share the results. As you dive deeper, you will begin to ask more questions and become more committed to improvement having now done the tough work. Being measurable will help you see risk, do not set boundaries.

For several years, our company has implemented EOS (Entrepreneurial Operating System). EOS is an organizational structure and team approach which perfectly suits the contingent litigation law firm. EOS subscribes to the right person right seat approach to running any business. EOS is a proven program that will help establish the vision, discipline, and focus necessary to at a minimum transform the way you do subrogation in your law firm. Look to your employees for GWC, do they Get it, Want it, and have the Capacity to do the job.

Lastly, time is a bonafide enemy of the contingent law firm. It quietly erodes dollars and the goodwill of a job well done. Law firms spend a tremendous amount of money to get a client, make sure you are doing everything you can to protect that investment.

Todd Franklin is CEO and Legal Strategist for MASSIVE: Medical and Subrogation Specialists is an expert in pinpointing issues and problem-solving. He most recently helped pioneer our proprietary case management software system CTS to help law firms efficiently resolve medical lien claims made against personal injury settlements of any kind.

Todd continues to produce measurable results using disciplined and documented systems. Having helped tens of thousands of clients receive the advocacy they deserve and through an understanding of the subrogation difficulties trial lawyers face daily; Todd is often sought to speak at legal industry events across the United States. He continues to exceed expectations in helping law firms efficiently navigate the maze of lien resolution.

Chapter 11

MARKETING TO THE SPANISH MARKETPLACE

Liel Levy

Co-founder Nanato Media

At my agency, Nanato Media, our main focus is helping law firms meaningfully market to their local Hispanic community. I always stress "meaningfully" because we do so much more than just take their English ads and translate them. *Meaningful* marketing includes understanding ambicultural distinctions that speak to and engage Hispanic prospects.

PROS AND CONS: of Advertising Before COVID-19

Pros

It should come as no surprise that the biggest pro of legal advertising *before* COVID-19 is that it was *a lot* easier. Many firms enjoyed successful marketing campaigns even if they weren't customized to different cultural segments. Sure, they were leaving plenty of money on the table, but ignorance is bliss, especially when it's still profitable.

For years now, we've known that minorities don't want to get lumped in with the majority when it comes to marketing. They prefer brands – and, yes, your law firm is a *brand* – that proves they understand what makes them unique.

And, to be fair, *some* firms did that before COVID-19. It was just that there was so much business out there, many more firms could get away with just ticking the boxes. One landing page in Spanish? Check. English TV ads dubbed over for Spanish TV? Check. That's about all it took for a marketing campaign aimed at prospects to *look* successful.

Cons

Something very interesting happened to our industry once the COVID-19 lockdowns started. As you probably know, "essential" workers were still allowed to perform their jobs, albeit at the risk of catching the virus. Many of these essential workers were Latino. Many of these Latino essential workers didn't receive help from the government stimulus checks or access to healthcare. Other events over the past few months have also reignited old conversations about discrimination against minorities in America, including systems of exclusivity.

So, Latinos face greater levels of exposure because they make up greater numbers of essential workers, *but* they also face a harder time getting help because of structural systems that keep them out.

As a result, businesses – including law firms – need to rethink their messaging and adopt new strategies that prove to Hispanic Americans that they understand their cultures, including these pressing challenges. Relying on Spanish translations is no longer just a lackluster approach. It's a losing one that risks the business coming across as tone-deaf or even cold.

To me, this really isn't a "con." I'm not saying that as someone who owns a Hispanic marketing agency, either. I'm seeing it as a human being who lists progress under "pro." And companies looking below the surface of their markets is definitely progress.

HOW ARE THINGS CHANGING

A pessimist – or a "realist," as they're fond of calling themselves – might look at the current situation and say, "Yeah, but things will change when COVID is over."

Well, Zoom's stock prices beg to differ.

The millions of parents who have filed with the government for homeschooling do, too.

The countless companies making long-term plans for work-at-home arrangements are clearing their throats, as well.

Hispanic prospects are never again going to call attorneys who "made an effort" by running a poorly translated Spanish ad.

And that's because they won't have to. Hispanic Americans are the fastest-growing minority in our country. Currently, *37 million* people in our country are Spanish speakers. That number skyrocketed by *233%* between 1980 and 2013 and continues to grow.

So, firms can go back to ignoring this population's demands, but this population no longer needs to settle for being ignored.

FUTURE EXPECTATIONS

I don't need a crystal ball to show me what's coming. No matter where your firm is located, you're most likely near a large or growing Hispanic population. If you want any of their business going forward, you'll need a fully implemented bilingual and culturally relevant digital strategy.

Or, who knows? Maybe *not* making money will be fun, too.

As I've said, this kind of strategy needs to be thoughtful. Ads need to be relevant in terms of the services advertised, the language used, and the culture referenced. Remember: "Hispanic" is an umbrella term. Under that umbrella, there are Mexicans, Guatemalans, Dominicans, and dozens more with their own unique cultures and even unique versions of Spanish. Taking a "one-size-fits-all" strategy is taking no strategy at all.

If you take this kind of approach *and* pair it with community outreach and grassroots support, success is guaranteed. Best of all, Hispanics are fantastic about word-of-mouth. So, take the time to establish yourself as a legal advocate for your local Hispanic community and they will become your best marketers.

ADVICE MOVING FORWARD

Prioritize agility in your firm's marketing strategy. I can't emphasize enough how important it is to adopt the kind of strategy I just described, *but* I'd also be a hypocrite if I said the same exact approach will work for a firm in Los Angeles as it will for one in Detroit. Take the time to familiarize yourself with your local Hispanic community and fine-tune this strategy accordingly.

While I still recommend community involvement, face-to-face interactions don't need to be the norm anymore. Technologies like Facetime and Facebook Live make it possible to have sincere, engaging conversations with one prospect or dozens. Take advantage of that.

Speaking of agility *and* technology, leverage both to improve the customer experience you're able to provide. Either consistently innovate and improve or needlessly struggle. Traditionally, firms have been slow to adopt new technologies. *Some* – definitely not yours, I'm sure – aren't even digitized. If your firm isn't taking advantage of modern technology, it won't be agile enough for modern markets.

Finally, don't fear "the new normal." It's going to be full of promise, progress, and – if you use the type of marketing strategy I've described – profits.

Liel Levy's experience with marketing legal services to U.S. Hispanics began in childhood when he watched his uncle build one of the most prominent legal brands for injured Latinos in CA from the ground up. From promoting the brand at Hispanic community outreach events to doing intake for PI and WC to, most recently, opening new markets, Liel has seen and done it all. This includes a successful 12-year career in international luxury hospitality. In 2018, he co-founded Nanato Media. The agency offers bilingual marketing services aimed at Hispanic Americans. These services give law firms exponential business and brand growth and are delivered with outstanding customer service.

Chapter 12

MASTERMINDS: EXCEPTIONAL PIVOTING FOR POWERFUL RESULTS

Ken Hardison, Esq.

Founder & President of PILMMA (Personal Injury Lawyers Marketing & Management Association)

Many of the world's most successful business leaders and CEOs rely on Mastermind Groups to propel them forward and especially so when they are facing challenging times. Author Napoleon Hill originally coined the Mastermind concept in his 1925 book, *The Law of Success*. As Hill defines them, Masterminds are: "two or more people coming together in harmony to solve problems." But Mastermind groups are not just some arcane concept from a by-gone era. They remain cutting-edge tools that motivated lawyers leverage so they can experience dramatic growth and increased profits.

Participating in a Mastermind group is like having your private board of directors- with every member bringing fresh ideas, insights, and strategies to the table, and sharing them freely. The synergy of compounded intellect within a quality Mastermind group is unparalleled.

Each member raises the bar for the other members. Entrepreneur Jim Rohn states it this way: " You are the average of the five people you spend the most time with." Success truly breeds success.

After spending over 20 years participating in and facilitating over 250 Mastermind meetings, I can honestly say that there is no substitute for Masterminds in helping motivated lawyers experience exponential growth. Back when I was still practicing law, my firm grew an astounding 1600% from 1998-2003, once I joined a Mastermind group! And over the years, as I've facilitated Mastermind groups with lawyers all across the country, I've continued to see lawyers experience dramatic growth, time and time again.

In traditional Mastermind meetings, each member takes turns presenting the marketing and management strategies that they have been working on recently or since the last meeting. They share what has proven successful, including specific strategies, techniques, helpful vendors, etc. Just as importantly, they also share challenges or obstacles they face and gain insight, suggestions, and ideas from their fellow members. Invariably, there will be round-table discussions on a variety of relevant subject matters, such as how to pay associates, how to scale a law firm, how to systematize one's firm, etc. Sometimes leading industry leaders or thought leaders speak to the group, and they will teach a crucial concept or strategy, and members are allowed and encouraged to pick their brains in this small setting.

During Covid-19, I've seen even more interest in and participation from Mastermind members than ever before! Members are eager to brainstorm on the litany of new challenges the pandemic has created for law firms. During any crisis, successful lawyers must be prepared to PIVOT- to change course quickly and strategically so that they continue to steer their ships forward. Masterminds have allowed lawyers to PIVOT their marketing and operations during Covid-19 better. In weekly virtual meetings, I've seen my Mastermind members provide invaluable support to one another. Together, they've tackled issues such as 1) Going Remote, 2) Managing Remote Employees, 3) Marketing tactics and Negotiating

Media Buys to obtain more bang for their advertising bucks during Covid-19, 4) Creating PSA's and more pronounced Social Media Presence since potential clients are spending more time than ever online, 5) Exploring and Diversifying into New Practice areas, such as Business Interruptions Claims, Debtor-Creditor Law and Bankruptcy(all areas that law firms should be looking at during COVID), 6) Community Involvement Ideas like Giving Away Face Coverings and Bottles of Sanitizer, and 7) PPP SBA Loans and 8) Strategies and Checklists for Reopening Procedures during Covid-19.

One of the keys to a successful Mastermind is having an experienced facilitator who sets the agenda and keeps the meetings moving. They should engage those members who are less vocal and respectfully by firmly quiet down the members who are too vocal or monopolize the group. It also helps if the facilitator is an expert in the field that he or she is facilitating. In some respects, the Mastermind facilitator is like an orchestra leader who helps the various instruments come together effectively to produce the music of the Mastermind.

It's also essential that the Mastermind facilitator place members in the specific group that will be most beneficial both for the individual member's growth, as well as the mutual edification of the group at large. For example, I strive to create the right "fit" within each Mastermind group I facilitate. Novices do not need to be in the same group with those whose firms are larger or who are more adept at navigating the complexities of digital marketing. Their pressure points and challenges differ too drastically. While there is much to learn in each group, optimal placement ensures that the members are "equally yoked." Otherwise, members feel dissatisfied, and the exchange of ideas doesn't work as well.

Why do Masterminds work so well in driving lawyers to greater success? If you think about it, you know that different people have different strengths and life experiences. Each member of a Mastermind brings their unique perspective to the table, and the result is a sum that is greater than its parts. One member's fresh insights or ideas will spark another member's ideas. Masterminds are also gathering places for like-minded individuals. There is undeniable power in spending intentional time with other successful, like-minded and motivated law firm owners for support, clarity, motivation, and to jumpstart one's law firm marketing and management with fresh ideas and insights.

Successful Law Firm owners also leverage Masterminds as a means of speeding implementation. By drawing on the brain-power of the collective group- you can identify winning strategies and weed out time and money wasters. You are better able to eliminate blind spots and create shortcuts because you learn from one another's mistakes and take advantage of lucrative opportunities others in the group have discovered. It's like having 10-12 times the individual brain-power, laser-focused on finding solutions for law firm challenges.

In the current environment of unpredictability, some lawyers are pulling back, laying off employees, and making cuts in marketing expenses- But successful lawyers seeking to PIVOT forward during this crisis are doubling down on their marketing. You must strive to maintain a proactive vision for your firm rather than a reactionary one. Look for strategies that will propel your firm forward both now and when this pandemic subsides. Don't fall into a conservative short-term mode of decision making from the point of fear or worry that will ultimately short circuit your future opportunities for growth and continued success.

I'm not advocating that you ignore the realities we are all facing as business owners, including keeping an eye on the financial bottom line. But I am suggesting that whatever decision you make- whether to become smaller and leaner or to go aftermarket domination with increased advertising aggressively buys in TV, Radio, PPC, Facebook Ads, and so forth. The key is to ask yourself why you are making specific decisions at this time. Successful firm owners are always seeking to move their business forward, even when facing difficulties or uncertainty.

Instead of paralysis, PIVOT! Make an intentional mindset shift. Look for new ways to improve productivity and efficiency. Explore new potential practice areas, such as bankruptcy, debtor-credit law, business interruption claims, etc. Focus renewed energy on management to increase accountability, motivation, and productivity. Take advantage of current market conditions to more aggressively dominate your market through continued advertising. Spend time making sure you have a systematized means of nurturing and following up on fence-sitting leads with email drip campaigns, books, written reports to share with them systematically. Use the top-of-mind marketing tactics to convert leads to clients. These are the very concepts and strategies being discussed right now by Mastermind members all across the country.

While it's easier to be successful when the economy is roaring, and there is no disruption, great law firms and business owners know how to survive and move forward in times of crisis like those facing lawyers today. Masterminds are a conduit for helping lawyers PIVOT during adversity and experience continued growth and professional advancement

Looking back, I can say that there's no way I would be where I am today if it had not been for the various Masterminds I've been in since the late '90s. At present, I facilitate five different Law Firm Owner Mastermind groups and am personally involved in 2 non-attorney entrepreneur Masterminds with business owners from all over the world. There is no substitute for the power of a Mastermind, and I encourage you to explore the possibility of joining a Mastermind or forming your own Mastermind- especially during a time in which lawyers all across the country are facing the unique challenges presented by Covid-19.

Ken Hardison has fought for people's rights as a trusted personal injury lawyer for over 35 years. His ethics, integrity, and passion for his clients helped to build one of North Carolina's most successful firms, Hardison & Cochran, and a successful Social Security disability firm, Carolina Disability Lawyers, in Myrtle Beach, South Carolina. Now, as founder and president of PILMMA, Ken devotes his time to helping attorneys build their own preeminent law practices with proven marketing strategies and management resources. Ken has built and mentored successful

Mastermind Groups for lawyers from across the country. He has been recognized as one of the top 100 Trial Lawyers in North Carolina and is a member of the exclusive Million Dollar Advocates Forum. He's the author of many books, including *Systematic Marketing, Under promise Over Deliver,* and his latest book *Powerful Online Legal Marketing.* He is a sought-after speaker throughout the country on marketing and managing law firms. Ken is known as the "Millionaire Maker" because he has helped so many lawyers double, triple, or quadruple their law practices and income by following Ken's practical Strategies for Law Firm Growth and Success. Ken lives in Myrtle Beach, SC, where he enjoys playing golf and fishing when he is not helping lawyers grow their practices.

Chapter 13

PAY PER CLICK

Jarred Johnson

President and CEO of Sue The Collector & PPCSquared.com

PPC Ads (or Pay Per Click) for Law Firms has always been one of the hardest, most competitive ad spaces in Digital Marketing. Google has ranked Legal advertising as one of the top three most expensive clicks year after year, with per click costs exceeding $500+. With escalating costs, you cannot afford to make a mistake, as mistakes can cost you millions.

Because of the COVID pandemic, Law Firms have doubled down on their budgets, spending even more money than usual to attract and retain new clients for various plaintiff campaigns. We've seen almost every segment of plaintiffs' marketing go up in the past year. Everything from Motor Vehicle Accidents to various mass torts campaigns, the costs are higher than ever. The bottom line is still 80/20. 80% of your new clients will only ever come from 20% of your keywords. A skilled PPC manager will work daily to figure out what 20% of your keywords will generate the exact cases you are looking for, and in turn the 80% of your waste search keywords off. Most simply do not spend the time or don't have a process in place to eliminate those wasteful keywords and that is the only reason why your campaign is not performing as you'd expect and why your costs in a particular case are too high.

Back when I built my very first campaigns for a Personal Injury law firm in Los Angeles, I wanted to know what people in a motor vehicle accident were searching for and what they were not. Getting into the "conversation" inside your ideal consumer's head is absolutely key to discovering the 20% and eliminating the 80%. The easiest way to figure it out, is to ask people you meet on the street, in an Uber, or in an elevator, *what would they do if they were in a car accident and needed a lawyer?* The answers I discovered all centered around one theme and not too surprisingly, the answers were a by-product that personal injury TV and Radio ads were directly responsible for.

I asked a hotel bellhop a simple question in Irvine, California, "If you were hurt today on the job, who do you call?" Without hesitation, two bellhops sang a jingle they knew by heart to me in Spanish "Call 1-800-636-3636," which is the number for Los Defensores®, a major advertising firm in Los Angeles owned by Mary Ann-Walker of Walker Ads. If they didn't know the number, they would have Googled "Los Defensores," instead of "Abogado Accidentes" or "Car Accident Lawyer" or something basic. They have already been thoroughly indoctrinated because of their radio that plays all day, at their bellhop desk outside the Hyatt Regency, which plays the Los Defensores spot 12 times a day.

This intelligence on what these specific consumers would reference right away if they were in a bad accident or hurt at work is the 20% of keywords that makes up a campaign. It's not common for most consumers these days to not have been exposed to some form of TV or Radio advertising, and your ideal consumer will use their phone to Google the name or brand they remembered to try to reach out. This phenomenon is uniquely specific to personal injury clients as personal injury lawyers have spent billions to make their brand in their hometown the most famous, most recognized name in town, and in doing so, has erased all other firms from existence. When a consumer needs to do some research on those big brands and big firms, it's your chance to insert yourself in the conversation, using Google Ads.

PROS AND CONS:

The PROS of running a Google Ad to find new cases for your law firm are simple, if you can discover the right keywords that your ideal consumer is using, you can bid on those searches and present your legal services to the consumer for as little as $.01 per click. You can have an ad up and running in less than 5 minutes, and new clients coming in the door the same day.

The CONS are very simple, Google only allows for a very small window to have your ad seen, often referred to as the "Google 3 pack", or the top three (or four) spots in a particular search on its Search Marketing platform. The costs to maintain an ad within the top three spots, even if you have the highest possible quality score in the platform can still be very cost-prohibitive, simply because your competition is bidding extremely high bids to achieve those coveted top spots. If you're not willing to wager those same or similar amounts, your ad won't be noticed by over 90% of the search traffic for that particular search term you are bidding on.

HOW ARE THINGS CHANGING:

Google for the past five years has progressively been marching towards one thing, fully automated ads. You tell Google what your ideal conversion looks like, and Google runs the ads for you, setting the bids, budgets and all to help you achieve your goals. The truth about this "total automation" fairyland story is the only goal Google is going to achieve is siphoning more money out of your pockets. The more features Google has taken away over the years has all universally benefited Google and never the end-user or the advertising agency managing the ads.

Google has taken dozens of controlling features away, many of which have had devastating effects on your ability to stay within budget and keep your costs in check. One of these features was "Daily Budget." For almost 15 years, if you set a daily budget for a particular campaign in Google, Google would not exceed that budget. If it did, it simply would not charge you for the over delivery in ads. Now, Google will exceed your daily budget up to 4 times the amount you specify in the platform. The only workaround available is to install a custom JavaScript into Google Ads to monitor and shut down a campaign that exceeds its budget. If you don't have this solution built into all your campaigns, you risk spending all your budget in the first half of the month and having no budget left the rest of the month. Who benefits? Google. What's Google's mantra? "Never Be Evil". When you consider how specific this change was made and why, their mantra is laughable. Bottom line, Google will continue to change its platform to benefit them. Best to stay on top of hacks and scripts that will reign in their corporate greed.

FUTURE EXPECTATIONS:

Google will continue to implement changes to its platform to benefit itself first. New search engines are trying to break through and offer some amount of competition, like DuckDuckGo and Microsoft Ads with BING. Google will continue to dominate this marketplace for years to come but it has slowly lost a ton of ground to another very well-known company a few miles away from the Googleplex on Hacker Lane, namely, Facebook. Facebook has started to branch its platform into more of a resource for its users, and Facebook knows that its users spend way more time on its platform vs. Google. That prolonged attention on the Facebook platform gives Facebook a lot of interesting data that it, in turn, uses to market "products of interest" to its users. Because Facebook isn't a Google Auction, it favors the advertiser that can create the right ad, that attracts the most favorable feedback from its user base, and in turn shows that ad more often based on positive data received. This data is key to seeing a Facebook ad perform well. At some point, Google will push to revamp its ratings and rankings in a similar way.

ADVICE MOVING FORWARD:

You can compete! Even if you are a tiny firm, with a tiny budget to spend on ads, you need to focus your money and media purchases on standing right up against the largest firm in town. The key to success is within the 80/20 principle of advertising. When you can focus your campaign, keywords and text ads to capture the fleeting attention of 20% of searches that actually result in a sign-up, you will grow your firm and start to make serious money. Plenty of fly-by-night Ad agencies come and go, so always GET A REFERENCE from firms that have used that specific ad agency before handing over hard-earned cash. You may only have enough money to get it right once, so be cautious and use prudence in hiring the right ad manager. The right ad manager will have decades of experience and know all the major players well within your local market.

Jarred D. Johnson has been managing PPC for Lawyers since 2003, obtaining individual certifications with Google for the past decade, and also obtaining Premier Partner status with Google with his company PPC² Digital Marketing for Law Firms. He also owns and co-founded one of the largest consumer law brands in the nation, namely Sue The Collector. He's managed millions of dollars in ads for over 100 different law firms over the past decade and has worked on the front lines to develop new strategies to get the right traffic for his clients. His focus has always been to find the niche in a particular campaign, so his company does not have to compete with other firms that go after the lowest hanging fruit.

Chapter 14

STATE VS. FEDERAL

Ruth Rizkalla

Co-founder and head of Kirtland &
Packard LLP's Mass Tort Department

COVID and its continuing aftermath has undoubtedly changed the practice of law, from how we interact with our clients, to how we litigate and try cases; to administrative changes within our firm. I was at the airport in Jacksonville, flying home from the PGA Championship when I received emails that California was on lockdown and schools and workplaces were shutting down to prevent the spread of COVID. The safety measures instituted shortly thereafter were truly dystopian as the world went through a never-before-seen situation.

Even after practicing law across 50 states in both state courts and federal courts for over 17 years, nothing could have prepared me for this. What follows is an outline of some of the changes that have taken place in state courts and federal courts post-COVID, as well as for lawyers and law firms in the practice of law itself.

COVID's Effect on State and Federal Courts and the Way We Litigate:

State and Federal Courts nationwide have implemented a series of rules to help curb the spread of COVID in their courtrooms while attempting to provide justice and adjudication of issues and claims. Both state and federal courts are bobbing and weaving in response to COVID's considerable onslaught, and so far they are doing quite the stellar job of adapting and balancing the needs of all involved.

Some state courts will only hold remote hearings while others only allow hearings with social distancing provisions or only if they have been deemed as essential or emergency matters. California State Courts, for example, have delayed filings in every city and county. In the Superior Court, County of Los Angeles, all civil jury trials are continued until January 2021, but criminal trials will go forward due to defendants' rights to Speedy Trial under Penal Code Section 1382. Such rules ensure the safety of parties, lawyers, judges, juries and court staff, meanwhile ensuring that all parties' grievances are heard, with priority and special attention given to cases that need it most.

Federal Courts have also adapted to the post-COVID world, and have been creative with protocols for conducting jury trials. For instance, the United States District Court of the Southern District of California holds in-person trials with a protocol that consists of 25 written concepts on how the trials are to take place. These written concepts are designed and drafted to balance the rights of the parties to have their grievances and defenses heard, with the health and safety of all participants. On the other hand, The United States District Court of the Central District of California takes a different approach than its sister court in the Southern District. The Central District allows individual judges to offer bench trials by video conference only, disallowing all in-person trials for both civil and criminal matters. Federal Courts have also given priority to criminal cases due to the Speedy Trial Act.

As we continue to practice law in the shadows of the pandemic, we should expect to adapt ourselves as new blows continue to be dealt. For instance, recently in California, Governor Gavin Newsome announced a revised budget that proposes funding reductions of 10% to court operations to offset the State's COVID-inflicted deficit of $54 billion. As most lawyers and judges are already feeling the strain of overloaded dockets and delayed proceedings, it is grim to imagine the negative impact of a large-scale budget cut.

COVID's Effect on the Practice of Law Itself:

COVID's effects on the practice of law are multifaceted and can be hard to predict. As counterintuitive as it seems, COVID can have surprisingly positive effects. For instance, it can boost demand for legal advising in some sectors involving personnel directly exposed to the virus, such as essential workers. Law firms can provide companies and corporations with information on how to treat employees who have been infected with COVID, or advise their clients on the Centers for Disease Control and Prevention's constantly updated guidelines. Law firms that represent individuals may also find an uptick in business due to violations of law based on employers not providing reasonable accommodations or responding appropriately to employees who are at high risk for severe illness if they contract COVID.

Moreover, COVID has inspired a whole new generation of claims. Recently, plaintiffs lawyers representing hundreds, if not thousands of plaintiffs nationwide, attempted to persuade the Judicial Panel on Multidistrict Litigation that insurance claims for business interruptions stemmed by COVID should be consolidated into one court before one judge. Although the petition for consolidation was denied, the existence of this petition and the sheer number of plaintiffs marks the beginning of what will surely be different waves of litigation spawned by and directly related to COVID.

Unfortunately, the reality is that most lawyers and firms are hurting financially, just like the majority of businesses in the reeling economy resulting from COVID. Law firms have been shutting down offices due to known infections of employees to halt the spread of the virus. Some firms have closed offices completely and shifted to remote working. In order to keep their business afloat, firms have also slashed their payrolls and laid-off workers.

For all firms, adapting their practice is essential, at least until COVID has mostly subsided. Until then, lawyers and law firms must embrace the continuous changes brought about by the pandemic, both unexpectedly positive and unpredictably negative.

Last Words:

As I am the eternal optimist, I know that we lawyers will make it past the chaos COVID has brought. By nature and profession, we are both diligent and persistent. Equally as important as making it past the chaos, we must make the most of our practice during the chaos. We do it for our families, our friends, our clients and ourselves. We have to.

Ruth Rizkalla has been practicing law for 17 years, focusing on complex litigation - primarily mass tort litigation/pharmaceutical litigation. She is the Co-founder and head of Kirtland & Packard LLP's Mass Tort Department and in charge of all aspects of that practice. Kirtland & Packard LLP was founded in 1932 and has extensive experience in multi-party and multidistrict litigations, beginning with MDL-13 in 1967. Ms. Rizkalla has litigated and served as leadership in multiple California Judicial Council Coordinated Proceedings (JCCPs) and Multidistrict Litigations (MDLs) for mass tort litigations. She has been appointed Co-Liaison Counsel in the *In Re Zoloft Birth Defect Cases*, JCCP 4771; Co-Liaison Counsel in the *In Re Cymbalta Withdrawal Cases*, JCCP 4825; Co-Lead Counsel in the *In Re Xarelto Products Liability Cases*, JCCP 4862; and Plaintiff's Steering Committee member in the *In Re Pradaxa Products Liability Cases*, JCCP 4863; and Plaintiff's Steering Committee member in the *In Re 3M Combat Arms Earplugs*, MDL 2885. She has represented many thousands of plaintiffs in both state and federal courts nationwide.

Chapter 15

TOLL-FREE/VANITY NUMBERS

Paul Faust

President and Co-founder of RingBoost

One of the many lessons we have learned during the Covid-19 pandemic is the Power of Voice. When times are tough, stressful and people are looking to connect they don't yearn for a text message or an email or a web form. They want to hear Your Voice. They want to connect in a personal way, with emotion, intonation and personalization. That is the power of Your Voice and our numbers can help you do that.

This is certainly most true for law firms. People are scared and they don't have the ability to connect in the face-to-face ways they did before. Being able to speak to an attorney who can empathize and guide them through their legal issue is critical. There is NO BETTER WAY to do this than via a phone call.

Voice connection remains the most efficient and powerful tool for law firms to turn inquiries into clients. The world - business and personal - runs on mobile. Inbound calls are shown to convert to revenue 10-15 times greater than web leads, with an average of 28% greater revenue. A memorable local or toll-free number can help do this. It is one important tool in the marketing mix that should not be overlooked.

Whether during these unprecedented times or during more normal times, attorneys spend considerable time and money focusing on how they will stand out, how they will market/advertise and build their businesses. From websites, to social media, TV, radio and billboards, taglines and community initiatives...in a highly competitive industry...standing out can make the difference between success and failure. No matter how much people spend on their advertising and marketing efforts, they cannot replicate who you are. The quicker you can connect with a potential client via the phone, the quicker you can build a connection and show them that you can give them the help they need. They are no longer just a "webform," an "inquiry"....they are an individual with a serious need and you can be there to help them.

With today's rapidly changing technology there will be ever-increasing new digital marketing tools, algorithm changes, apps, social media sites and programs, artificial intelligence chat tools and on and on. Attorneys will need to be or will need to hire experts to stay on top of the latest trends and will need to try and test everything. The use of a phone number hasn't changed and EVERYONE knows how to make a call. This tried-and-true tool should be part of every firm's marketing/advertising mix.

Paul Faust is President and Co-Founder of RingBoost, the nation's largest specialty phone number company including local, toll-free, vanity, easy-dial, tracking numbers, and exhausted area codes. A recognized industry leader, Paul organized the first conference for phone number providers in 2010 and has been a featured speaker at many telecom conferences, including the Somos Toll-Free User Summit. Paul has been active in the legal marketing industry for almost 15 years and was inducted to the PILMMA Hall of Fame in 2017. Paul attends 10-12 legal conferences per year as either an attendee or exhibitor and has worked with hundreds of law firms across the country. He has been featured in dozens of legal and entrepreneur blogs and podcasts and is currently a member of the Mass Tort Vendor Association and Trusted Legal Partners Group.

Chapter 16

SINGLE EVENT/MASS TORTS/ CLASS ACTION

Steven Gacovino, Esq.

Founding Partner - Gacovino Lake & Associates PC

Gacovino, Lake & Associates, P.C. is in Sayville, NY (Long Island, NY), and so being in New York, our office immediately went remote. Particularly, as New York was identified as one of the most COVID-affected states, we acted quickly to keep everyone safe and out of the office, but still stay connected.

Regarding cases, single events came to a halt because there was no human activity. Normal daily activities like walking and driving slowed down considerably and so slip and falls or car accidents no longer happened. However, mass tort advertising did well because people were captive at home watching TV, on their social media, on their computers and we were able to sustain through the most difficult part of the pandemic. As such, mass tort case procurement has gone virtually uninterrupted and, in fact, during the worst part of the pandemic potential clients were more attentive to commercials.

The other thing that occurred was local courts launched themselves into the 21st century after being locked into the 20th century for a very long time. Courts were open using remote conferences and clients understood they might have to do remote depositions. It appeared to work out well for all parties involved. Today's technology opens the door for at least this part of the justice system to be much more efficient. However, there have been few, if any, jury trials in the immediate location of New York. Courts are still trying to see how to handle these court proceedings.

During the pandemic I was alone in the office and so after some time missed the organic interaction with others. Additionally, I initially felt that in-person interaction was quicker than having to track people and it was easier to speak to teams and individuals in the office. However, it did provide the opportunity to focus, without distractions, on our current cases. We had several Microsoft team phone calls throughout the week. We would section people off into teams to handle specific cases. As an example, for IVC filter cases, we had a team and sub-team for those cases to address and work on the case as a group and sub-group. By breaking them out into teams and utilizing them together with sub-teams, we were able to focus more on the cases. While the team has been away from the office there seems to be more accountability from home and Microsoft Teams has made it effective to have meetings. I have been able to review hundreds of cases together with my team.

As part of the adaptation due to COVID, we took advantage of courts shutting down and because of the pause in courts, no motion practices, and stays on statutes of limitations, we were able to play more offense on our current single event cases. We were also able to focus on clients and more day-to-day operations. We also focused more on front-end work. We took a lot of time to work on the cases we already had, so we came out of the pandemic with more and better cases, as well as in a better place as a law firm.

Steven Gacovino, Esq. received a Bachelor of Arts in political science in 1988 from the State University of Stony Brook before earning his degree in law from the Touro College Law Center in 1992. After graduating from law school, he became a founding partner of Gacovino Lake & Associates PC. Today, Steven Gacovino leads a team of New York personal injury attorneys, providing clients with the skilled, knowledgeable representation they need to obtain a favorable settlement or verdict. Steven Gacovino is admitted to practice law in the Federal District Courts of New York and Connecticut. His areas of practice include personal injury, wrongful death, criminal defense, will and estates and real estate law. Steven Gacovino remains active in the legal community and is a member of multiple professional organizations.

Chapter 17

PUBLISHING A BEST SELLING BOOK FOR MORE LEADS & CREDIBILITY

Cris Cawley

Founding Partner - Game Changer Publishing

L awyers writing books is certainly not a new concept. Let's be honest... If you can write a legal brief, you can publish a book. But why should you? There are many benefits to lawyers publishing a book to become the "go-to" expert in your niche. It's not as hard as it may sound, and when done the right way, it only requires a few hours of your time.

The easiest and quickest way to write a book is as follows:

1. Create a very detailed and granular outline on the subject that you want to speak about.

2. Speak and record the book over Zoom.

3. Transcribe the audio.

4. Have the book professionally edited and then formatted for digital and paperback layouts.

5. Create an award-winning cover.

6. Go to print.

7. Launch your book to the world!

While it may sound daunting at first, working with the right publisher can help you accomplish the entire process in 60-90 days. Most of the process beyond recording your content is completely done for you and again, when you publish a book the right way, you are only looking at approximately 4-6 hours of your time to collaborate on an outline and then to voice record your core content. This content will become the initial version of your manuscript.

When it comes to the book publishing industry, there is a *new* way and an *old* way. The old way is slow, you have zero control of the final outcome or your royalties, there is no built-in marketing to help the book actually sell copies after launching and there is no access to the names, emails or contact information of the people that buy your book. If you follow the new publishing model and do things the right way the first time, you pay a one-time upfront fee, you have full control over all elements of the publishing process, full control of your book and intellectual property. You also are not splitting your royalties with a publisher and the marketing is built into the book and launch process up front so it becomes a lead generator for your practice and a marketing tool that you can use long term to drive leads to your firm.

You may be asking, "But do I really need to write a book? How will that help grow my law practice?" Lawyers and professionals write books for many reasons–in rare cases it is a bucket list or legacy project, or someone just wants bragging rights. However, for those lawyers that "get it" on the business side of things, they quickly recognize the business advantages that come from writing a book which are as follows:

1. **More Authority.** A published book containing your expertise and specialized knowledge regarding a specific or area of practice positions you as the "go-to expert" or "authority figure" in your niche. A published book creates a perception of authority in the eyes of your potential clients.

2. **An Introduction.** A book serves as a simple but credible way to introduce potential clients to the pain points and solutions your firm offers that are related to their legal challenges. A potential client can purchase a paperback version or download the Kindle or digital version of your book on Amazon.com or on your website. This allows them to learn the basics of your subject matter and discover how it is pertinent to their individual situation, while gaining an understanding of the next steps on consulting or hiring an attorney for help.

3. **More Leads.** A published paperback book is a great "lead magnet" with built-in credibility. Whether you offer the digital version of your book on your own website as a download or sell your book online through Amazon or Barnes and Noble, the book can lead more clients to you and generate more quality leads for your practice.

4. **More Money.** The biggest reason people write books is to make more money. Publishing a book is something you do one time, but you can monetize forever or for as long as the content is relevant. You can then sell that book, which only took you hours to create, over and over long term. Not only are you generating income from book royalties, but you are also driving clients to your practice through the book, which is where the real money is made. This strategy can generate even more backend income in your business, when done the proper way.

5. **More Credibility.** Publishing a book brings more credibility to the author, which in turn leads to more impact and influence amongst your peers and in your space. If you're running a business and you publish a book with great content or a book that offers a solution to your target audience's biggest problems, this helps potential prospects understand who you are, how you can help and what your firm can offer. Additionally, your business and your name gain significant credibility,

especially if the book becomes a bestseller. Most new authors don't realize or believe how easy it is to publish a bestseller that gains a tremendous amount of respect from peers and fellow industry experts. It's quite simple, however. Publishing a bestseller comes down to the right kind of online marketing. It's simply about having the right funnel in place and driving targeted traffic to generate a significant number of sales in a short period of time. The top publishing companies know and understand this and incorporate it into their game plan upfront to ensure a successful book launch. A successful book also leads to speaking opportunities, podcast invites, media exposure and expert interviews, which also helps grow your business in other ways.

In 2006, Mike Schultz, principal of Wellesley Hills Group, released results from a survey of 200 business-book authors titled "The Business Impact of Writing a Book." In a follow-up article in *Businessweek* that same year, Schulz said, "The vast majority of the authors we surveyed -- 96% said they did realize a significant positive impact on their businesses from writing a book and they would recommend the practice."

There is no question that publishing a book is a great way to establish initial contact with potential prospects or business partners. Generally, those who try to cut corners on cost the first time around or self-publish and don't have a publisher to guide them through the maze of modern-day publishing, they don't spend money on marketing, they don't get invited to speak at conferences often, they sell way fewer books and they get much less backend benefit from the process. Doing it the right way, with the right publisher who knows and understands that the backend business that is generated from the book is just as important, if not more than selling the book itself initially, will benefit you in the short and long term. Regardless of your area of practice, publishing a book will help you grow your business and establish you as THE "go-to" expert in your field. There will never be a perfect time to write a book. That day will not come. You need to make up your mind to do it for your business and then enjoy the multi-faceted rewards long term. Stop thinking about it. Stop making excuses and invest money on the most valuable form of marketing there is for lawyers. One that will pay you back a return in many ways for years to come. Questions? Visit **www.PublishaBestSellingBook.com** or **www.CrisCawley.com** to learn more about our done-for-you book publishing solutions that will help you publish your book, get more leads, and be considered the "go-to" authority in your area of practice. You can also **schedule a free call here:** www.calendly.com/ccawley

Cris Cawley is the CEO of Game Changer Publishing, an award-winning consultant, successful marketer, and serial entrepreneur. She began her career in 1998 and has impacted over 155,000 entrepreneurs & professionals while helping them make a lasting impact on their industries through her book publishing, coaching, and private mastermind programs. Her best-selling programs teach her step-by-step proprietary systems to help clients leverage their knowledge, expertise, and passion into profits through high ticket programs & book publishing. She's been featured on many stages alongside some of the country's most sought-after speakers, influencers, and thought leaders. She has a passion for helping entrepreneurs and experts make a positive impact on the world and scale their businesses.

THE INTERVIEWS

Chapter 18

IT/SALES TECH

Nathan Cucciarre

President of N8 Solutions, N8 Development,
and N8 Specialized Transportation

Tell us your experience regarding the subject matter and pros and cons with regard to lawyer advertising prior to COVID and now.

Law firms are more open to marketing and sales messages that will enable them to quickly adapt to new ways of working, such as remote work. It's an area that firms are unfamiliar with, so they're more attentive to learning about new solutions.

IT teams and law firms have been under a lot of pressure, so it's not always easy to get hold of the right people during this time.

What's your view of the subject matter with regard to helping law firms prior to COVID and now and what kind of projections do you have for the future?

The goal of helping law firms hasn't changed because of COVID. Technology is an ever-changing environment already. The pandemic brought many things to light in common terms that people understood that IT has likely been preaching for a long time. If anything, the pandemic has galvanized the values in IT that we live by. The purpose of technology is to enhance the business efficiency while securing the data and communications it operates on.

The rapid transition to remote work has pushed law firms to quickly implement remote work solutions, which has surfaced a lot of cybersecurity issues. A great example is Zoom, which saw a 535% increase in daily traffic, but also emerged from the pandemic with an unwanted reputation for security and privacy lapses[1].

Prior to the pandemic, law firms were traditionally slow to adopt new technologies. However, the pandemic has forced many law firms to re-evaluate how they use technology to enable more flexible, and secure, ways of working. Firms that we support were forced to take on changes like this rapidly. Most of our customers were able to seamlessly transition to remote work.

Law firms are now more aware of cybersecurity issues and are taking the steps to secure their organizations. At the same time, the pandemic has accelerated digital transformation for many firms, as they adapt to new ways of working.

---

[1] -https://www.theguardian.com/technology/2020/apr/02/zoom-technology-security-coronavirus-video-conferencing

What industry changes have you seen because of COVID and how should we pivot?

Remote work has become essential to continue operations. We have seen a crash course in firms understanding the need to have an infrastructure that allows for that. This also highlights the greater understanding for security. Increasing the number of remote workers also increases the security risks that arise. The rapid move to remote work has unsurfaced serious security and compliance concerns for firms, and firms will need to take the appropriate steps to ensure data security and compliance moving forward.

This also introduces the importance for new ways of working. While people in the IT industry have been experts in remote working for some time it has to be translated to other organizations that need it. With lawyers and clients both working remotely, firms have had to find new ways to work with clients and conduct business, which has traditionally relied on in-person meetings.

What do you see as likely changes and trends coming down the pipeline because of the above?

Changes that were accelerated by the pandemic are already starting to take shape. Their importance has been defined by the experience.

Business transformation - The pandemic has forced a traditionally in-office culture to a virtual work environment. Not only will law firms need to continue to find new ways to enable flexible work environments, but also need to find new ways of working with clients - whether they be through collaboration tools, automated portals or shifting to a virtual business model.

Investment in technology - To support a growing decentralized digital workforce, firms will increase their investment in technology and tech support to bridge the gap in the new post-pandemic reality. From more secure infrastructures and cloud-based technologies to security solutions and remote IT support - firms will accelerate their tech investment rather than pull back.

Accelerated digital transformation - The changes brought about from the pandemic are pushing firms to accelerate digital transformation and more quickly respond to changing work environments. Technology will develop at a far faster pace than forecast pre-pandemic and will push firms to re-evaluate and re-prioritize their internal projects to focus on how technology can enable them to better cope with the challenges ahead.

What would be your overall advice to other lawyers moving forward in today's business and economic climate?

Adapt - IT has been looked at as a cost center for a long time. Many have understood this to be a necessity specifically because of times like this. The ability to work remote securely has been thrust onto firms everywhere. It shows that we all must adapt to new ways of working. While you may be accustomed to working with clients face-to-face, to be successful post-pandemic, you'll have to adapt to new ways of working. Whether that means learning new technologies, changing your routine or finding new ways to work with clients–be adaptable.

Be Aware – Introduction of home networks for remote working adds a new layer to infrastructure everywhere. Organizations have been in charge of security and maintenance of the internal network. Now adding a non-managed set of infrastructure brings in challenges and decisions that need to be made. Cybersecurity has always been an ever-evolving concern. Cybercriminals are using work-from-home situations to lure unsuspecting victims with phishing campaigns, malware and other attacks. Now they have a new way to drop ransomware into your internal network. Learn cybersecurity basics, protect your passwords and install antivirus software, and take the steps required to keep secure in today's evolving threat landscape.

Innovate – Out of uncertainty comes innovation. Take the opportunity to re-evaluate how you can improve your daily work practices and better service clients using technology. This is an ongoing process in IT and I believe it has been forced to the law firm industry as well.

BIO: **Nathan Thomas Cucciare** is President of N8 Solutions, N8 Development, and N8 Specialized Transportation. His career has been defined by the opportunity to work with the best people and technology in the field. He has over 20 years of IT experience driven by a passion that proves to be invaluable. The secret recipe for success is understanding the needs of the client. As his father Tom says, "Perception is 90% of the game." When Nathan's not working, he's spending life with his amazing wife Tarra and four kids, Sofia, Dominick, Luca, and Rocco. They travel as often as possible. Their happy place is always visiting the mouse or a beach in Florida. Feel free to reach out to him via email to learn more - nate@n8its.com

Chapter 19

CONTENT (ORGANIC GOOGLE)

Alex Valencia

Co-Owner of WeDoWebContent.com

Tell us your experience regarding your topic and about the pros and cons regarding lawyer advertising prior to COVID and how it is now.

So our expertise is that we do web content and content marketing for law firms. We've been doing strictly content marketing for lawyers since 2008. The way content worked when we first started was much easier, not only in volume, but for any content optimization for specific keywords for a law firm, because the internet wasn't saturated yet. So I'd like to think that we started off in content marketing for law firms as pioneers because we were one of the first agencies creating content and creating content strategies for lawyers back then. If a lawyer wanted to rank for a personal injury lawyer or car accident lawyer, or mass tort or social security family law, it was much easier because we knew how to develop the content format. The content was optimized and put on a website, whether it was a WordPress site or a private platform, it was a lot easier to rank.

But around 2009- 2010, the (hashtag) #contentisking came out and Google announced, if you want your websites to rank, you need to create content. So you have companies from all over the world selling content to every client, not just lawyers, but in every industry. This is around the time you started noticing more blogging happening, more social posts happening, content posts, people selling blogging packages to people and selling different opportunities to write content. And then it got so saturated that the internet was saturated with low value information–it didn't have authority, it didn't have a lot of truth to it. So they pulled back and said, we're making content a little stricter. And what Google did was create an algorithm, I think it was Panda, don't quote me, I don't remember all the different algorithms, but they said they were going to hit content pretty hard, and a lot of websites dropped.

Fortunately for us, we were doing it correctly for a long time. So we didn't really get affected by it. But we did have to restructure how content strategies were written and how content strategies were developed and how content was written for law firms. So we started experimenting with longer content, frequently asked questions, less blogging, and more page content. And that grew from there and started enhancing that. Google wants more authority; they don't want specifically length. But compared to other competitors in your market, you want to associate and strategize based on what is currently ranking. So we developed a software that helps us analyze what the top 10 law firms are ranking for, how long they're ranking for, how long the content is and how many links are coming to it, to create a better page. So that's what's helped us continue moving forward. Not only that, but we also partner with a great SEO agency. Their strategies and our process and formula that we've built throughout the years for content has really helped with the marketing side of things for lawyers as far as organic content is concerned.

Post COVID It actually only enhanced that more. So during COVID, we got on a phone call in a webinar with the SEO agency and the idea was digital is going to be even stronger now because everyone's home. So the more content we publish, the more important it's going to be to produce not only written content, but also video and social content. You have to be out there more than you ever were. If you were doing one post a day, at that point, you might want to hit that two, three or more times. If you're doing only one or two pages a week, you want to hit five. You want to hit the market strong, because what you do now is what's going to be your pipeline for 2021. So organic takes a lot longer, but it's more of an asset- it's going to help you in the long run. So the work that people are putting in in 2020, although there was a big drop in cases, it's only going to secure their positioning in 2021.

What's your view of the subject matter with regard to helping law firms prior to COVID? And your projections for the future?

It's to continue creating content, whether it's video, which is easy from your home, while you're quarantining, or write as much as you can, specifically, on your subject, right to your audience. A lot of things attorneys don't understand is if you're a personal injury lawyer, you're typically writing to anyone between a fourth and eighth-grade reading level. So don't always write lawyer to lawyer or speak lawyer to lawyer, always speak to the person like you're training someone below your education level. Give them as much information as they need to pick up the phone and call. You're using content as a conversion funnel to draw them to pick up the phone and call because that's where your leads will take over and help secure that into a case. So prior COVID, you know, a steady amount of content, post COVID, a continued steady amount of content, but diversifying in different areas–email marketing, social media, ads, more blogging, more external blogging. A lot of people don't use LinkedIn to their best benefit, but there's a great opportunity on LinkedIn Pulse, to share your ideas, share what you do, share how you help clients, and use that as an engine for you to continue growing the content and the value of your law firm.

What industry changes have you seen because of COVID? And how should we pivot?

The industries that have grown surprisingly, or maybe not so surprising, are in our vertical. Lawyers, I think, took advantage of purchasing a lot of masks and antiviral spray to use to send to their clients as a branding opportunity. I think that was smart. I think going back to some grassroots marketing, some mail, touching the client more often, retaining the client, and looking for more referral business were some opportunities taken by lawyers.

So one of our clients had the opportunity to step back during COVID and really analyze the clients they had as opposed to concentrating on the clients they didn't have. In going out to get more, they worked harder on their current clients. They built a relationship, and continued working them as if they were the only client. It gives you more of an opportunity to build that referral partnership with them.

What do you see as likely changes and trends coming down the pipe because of the above?

Again, I think more people are taking strict action on digital. There were still a lot of lawyers that were doing stuff old school, a lot of lawyers still doing paid search, which is fine and is still part of digital marketing, but when you're doing paid search, and there's not a lot of traffic coming to you, it's kind of a waste of money. So organic is that aspect of your website where you're building an asset. And it's always there for you working 24/7. Whereas paid is a "turn on" and "turn off" marketing aspect, which was great, because it allowed you to stop when you needed to, and you knew the market was changing. But organic is always there, it's kind of having that 24-hour salesperson for you. So definitely pivoting into more of an organic presence and diversifying that. If you were doing 80% Pay Per Click before and 20% other methods may be making that 60/40 or 50/50, just concentrating more on organic so it protects you in the future.

What would be your overall advice to other lawyers moving forward in today's business and economic climate?

Diversify your marketing. In the last question, I failed to mention how important television and radio still are. I think there's a great opportunity there. I know a lot of people pull money out of it, but I think there's still a good opportunity for you to brand yourself. So if they're seeing you on television, they're hearing you on the radio or you have an authoritative website with a good amount of content that's answering everyone's question, then you're using your social media as a branding aspect and not just sharing information that they don't want. You're using it as branding and staying in people's faces and retargeting and remarketing people correctly.

That would be my advice, to continue diversifying. You can't put all your eggs in one basket. Our advice is if you know we can't help you out, 100% you know, we'd rather not take you on as a client. If you're going to do it in steps, you have to do something. If you have to make a decision, you have to choose one place that you're going to market. You have to figure out where that's going to turn the most ROI for you in the beginning, and then start using those benefits from the ROI that you've gained from it to reinvest into your business.

Anything else you would like to add?

The idea of not doing any content without a content strategy is very important to me. Nothing happens. SEO doesn't happen. Your digital marketing doesn't happen without a content strategy. I would think of that as the foundation of your digital marketing strategy for your website. A lot of clients will just get a website, hire an SEO agency, and the SEO agency recommends some content for ranking purposes, which is great, right? Those high-ranking pages are huge for generating business, but they're also very highly competitive. So what happens there is you don't have a foundation of different parts of content to help support those pages. Good, well written content that concentrates on injuries is not only creative, it goes after the high-ranking keywords that you may or may not have. It does a competitor analysis. Google's moved into frequently asked questions, which is part of the featured snippet (the zero position), you'll see some law firms that rank and the accordion part of that snippet, where they answer all the questions that so many people asked. And, they don't just put one website, they put different firms or companies that are answering those frequently asked questions. Having a good, intelligent Frequently Asked Questions section on your website that creates its own page of content, not an accordion, creates its own index page by Google and is part of a good strategy. If the attorneys have the time or associates have the time, I would consider them having a blog as well, where they're writing on the site. Even if it's just one a week, from each attorney, it's important to have their voice and branding their name, showing that they're talking about local things, which helps local presence as well. Google My Business is a huge tool for lawyers to have because they're local. They have local clients, and you're trying to hit a local market. So writing locally using Google My Business with imagery about your law firm or any posts that have things that you're doing locally in the area associated with that location is important to help your localized ranking.

To add a little bit more about mass tort. So we take on a lot of national personal injury lawyers, and local experts and injury lawyers. Don't be afraid if you have an authoritative site to add mass tort pages. We created something called a skyscraper page, which is anywhere from 2000 to 10,000 words on a specific tort that has helped a lot of our clients rank well, and generate a lot of their own organic leads locally. That helps not only with authority, but obviously growing and diversifying the firm. So using their personal injury site for generating mass tort leads and actually localizing those topics makes it very easy for someone to rank that's already ranking.

Alex Valencia is a successful entrepreneur, marketer, and president of We Do Web Content, an Inc. 5000 business. His firm devises content and marketing strategies and produces online content for law firms, medical professionals, and small businesses nationwide. Alex and his wife Yvette founded We Do Web Content in 2008, driven by three deeply rooted convictions. First, content is, in fact, the undisputed king—and this makes it an invaluable asset. Second, every business—not just deep-pocketed corporations—should enjoy access to such a vital asset. Third, any asset this mission-critical demands a serious, well-conceived strategy. These are the beliefs that propel Alex and that drive We Do Web Content. Alex has applied his passion for digital marketing and content strategy to catapult We Do Web Content far into the stratosphere of today's legal and medical industries. From 2018 to 2020, the firm saw explosive growth, increasing its staff size five times over and yielding a three-year growth of 197%. In 2020, We Do Web Content became a proud member of the <u>Inc. 5000</u>. Today, the firm continues on its exciting journey and is exploring a rebranding and expansion of services. Alex counsels hundreds of clients with the broad knowledge gained from his direct experience in digital marketing, SEO, email marketing, marketing automation, content marketing, and social marketing. He has deepened this knowledge over the years by becoming an authority in relationship building and retention, legal and medical marketing, law firm and medical professional SEO, and attorney and medical professional digital marketing. He is also an Infusionsoft expert, a keen negotiator, and fluent in English and Spanish. Alex is a frequent contributor to <u>Search Engine Journal</u> as well as a <u>Forbes</u> Council Member and contributor. He, of course, continues to run and build his We Do Web Content business. Alex currently lives with his wife, Yvette, and their two, extremely artistic sons in Plantation, Florida.

Chapter 20

SEO LINK BUILDING, BACKLINKS, ONSITE SEO

Jason Hennessey

CEO at Hennessey Digital

Tell us your experience regarding the subject matter. The pros and cons regarding lawyer advertising, prior to COVID and also now.

I've been basically reverse engineering Google, doing something called organic SEO since 2001. I started working in the legal field back in about 2008. And the subject is something that continues to evolve. So some of the strategies that worked back in 2008 might not work today in 2021. You know, the core principles of organic SEO are the same. But Google is constantly getting better and they hire more. They hire smarter engineers. And you know they're trying to fight people that are trying to game the system of Google. And so working with lawyers since 2008, there's three core principles that really kind of drive a good SEO strategy for law firms.

The first is making sure that you are taking care of the integrity of the site. So that means all of the technical elements that make up your website, that's really it. Google basically sends out crawlers to visit your website. The crawlers then continue to access one link and go to the next link, and then continue to follow the links of the whole website. And it's just trying to crawl what you have. They're looking at your images. They're looking at your text. They're looking at your PageSpeed. They're looking at the markup of the actual code. So it's critical to know that's a very important aspect of a good organic SEO strategy. And that's probably the one thing that most lawyers that are reading this book, can't do themselves. That's probably the one thing that you probably want to engage with somebody that has more expertise in that. And just because somebody is a web developer doesn't necessarily mean that they know organic SEO. I want to kind of make that distinction, because I see a lot of people make that mistake of, "Oh, yeah, my cousin does web development," and they hire them. But if they don't know SEO, it's kind of like a specialty. So that's the first component.

The second component is building, just writing content, you know, publishing content on a regular cadence. That is something that lawyers who are reading this book could do on their own if they've got the time to do it. I would argue that's probably not the best use of their time, but it is something that they could be doing. That's the only way really to drive more eyeballs to your website with an organic SEO strategy is by publishing more content. Google indexes the content, you start ranking for more keywords, and as you rank for more keywords, you get more traffic, which then leads to phone calls, and then cases.

The third major component of a good SEO strategy is building the popularity of your website. Google has this thing called PageRank that goes from zero to 10 and started back in 2008. It would display what your PageRank was, for every single page on the web. They've since taken away that transparency, but there is still PageRank assigned to every single page on a website. And so how you build your PageRank is by getting other websites to link back to you, which then bleeds over PageRank from their websites to your website.

So, if you do those three things, and you're consistent, you can compete in just about any industry. But the problem is if you're just getting started today, you're competing with people that might have been doing SEO for 20 years. But that's not really a long time. SEO has only really been a thing for that long. I got started, like in the late 90s. So there's still time to catch up.

What's your view of the subject matter with regard to helping law firms prior to COVID and now, and your projections for the future?

I would say prior to COVID, there were a lot more people that were just doing what appeared to be working with, let's just say their whole holistic marketing strategy. They're just kind of doing TV advertising, they're doing billboards, they're doing radio, they're doing some digital marketing. I think once COVID happened, people really started to try to attribute cases to the marketing channels, and I think they were able to see what was working and what was not working. In my experience, I've seen a lot of people reshuffle their budget to focus more on the digital marketing aspect.

I just got a call yesterday from somebody that told us that they're pulling the majority of their TV budget and putting it into the digital because digital is the future. Even in today's day and age, my kids don't watch TV like I did. They'll watch Netflix, and they'll watch Hulu and places like that. But, they're not the target audience that's home from work watching Judge Judy, on a Wednesday afternoon who might have been involved in some type of an automobile accident or even some of the mass tort stuff for that case.

So, that's just it, a lot has changed. But even before COVID happened, I think the path was kind of in this direction anyway. But I think COVID just made it that much clearer. It made people take action sooner because they had a lot more time, they weren't commuting back and forth to work. They had the time to kind of investigate some of the cases, because, don't get me wrong, everybody took a hit at COVID, right? So when you're used to a normal pattern of phone calls and growth, and all of a sudden, March 2020 comes along, and there's a thing called COVID, most people think, alright, is it going to be two weeks, a month, right? And here we are talking today, a year later. Most firms have started to recover, but pretty much everybody took a hit. People were scared. People didn't know what was happening. People were losing their jobs. People were dying, right? So everybody's just kind of had more time to stay laser-focused because you start to go into crisis mode. And you're looking at your analytics, you're looking at your TV and what used to work is not working anymore, and you're just scratching your head, and you're really leaning in and analyzing every piece of your business. But now I think most are in recovery. And I think digital marketing is the future, it really is.

What industry changes have you seen because of COVID and how should we pivot?

What is changing? I think like I was saying more people are kind of pulling out of some of the traditional advertising that they're used to. So taking more money out of the TV campaigns and putting it into digital. But the other thing that I'm seeing too is that more people are starting to become more educated in digital. I think if you have reached this chapter, in this book right now, and you're reading this, that's just evidence that you are trying to continue to be an autodidact and teach yourself something that might be uncomfortable to you.

I think that lawyers should know, they shouldn't have to do their digital marketing strategies themselves. But they should study it to a point where they can actually hold somebody, whether it's an individual or an agency, accountable to getting good results from within the budget that they're spending.

I'm in fact writing another book myself called *Law Firm SEO*. It's a full book that kind of goes into much greater detail than what I'm covering in this chapter. I'm doing that because of COVID. It's because more people are genuinely interested in learning more about these types of subjects. And it's just more a matter of accountability because people are spending so much money, even before COVID, they were spending so much money on advertising and digital marketing. The problem is, In most cases, they don't even know what they're spending money on.

What do you see as likely changes and trends coming down the pipe because of the above?

I think technology is going to advance a lot quicker. One of our clients just got one of the largest verdicts in history, he got a $410 million verdict, and it was on a Zoom call. So, I think there will be changes like that where things will be a little bit more virtual. I think you won't necessarily see law firms that have three stories in big buildings. You might see a corporate headquarters, but people are working more remotely. You will probably see some leniency within the court systems for people going to trial. You might even start to see a big change in the education system. These colleges are for-profit universities and I think there's going to be a radical change in that. Another thing too, is now in certain states like Arizona, they're allowing non-lawyers to actually own law firms–that's a huge change that has taken place. You might start to see Wall Street get into the legal sector, which is kind of scary to think about, but things are changing. Some people just are uncomfortable with change, but change is inevitable. It's for the better or for the worse, depending on your outlook on how you're looking at it. But, again, as far as bringing things back to this particular subject, I think digital marketing is the future. We're glued to our phones. We're glued to our computers. We consume most of our media on our phones and on our computers. More people today are watching more six-second TikTok videos than they are one-hour sitcoms. And that's our future generation. The baby boomers, the millennials, the Generation X, everybody's kind of growing out of what was normal. We're kind of left with my children, and people's grandchildren, and we have to see their daily habits, we have to study their daily habits, and that will predict the future for us.

What would be your overall advice to other lawyers moving forward in today's business and economic climate?

Selfishly, I'm gonna talk about focusing on digital marketing. If you have more knowledge in the digital marketing field, you can actually win a war with lawyers that have way bigger budgets. And I see that all the time. I'll get on a call with an attorney that has been a staple in the market, a personal injury attorney who has been a staple in the market for 30 years. They're all over TV, and they're all over billboards, and they're advertising everywhere, and buses are driving by with their faces on them, right? And then I'll get on a call with them because they want to talk about SEO. It's something that most of these attorneys have neglected for many, many years. But because they've neglected it, there are some savvy recent law school grads that are five years out of law school that started to read books on SEO and watch YouTube videos, and now they're actually taking more of the digital market share away from the big player, right? And so I'll get on a call with them. And I'll say, "Would you consider these two people your competitors?"

And they're like, "I never heard of that guy. I don't even know who they are."

And so just because you don't know who they are doesn't necessarily mean anything, because I discovered them by doing a search for a keyword that would be relevant to your business.

And so that's just a case in point. Sometimes it's the savviest marketers who are the best lawyers, according to Google. And these lawyers that are focused on learning and teaching themselves more about this digital marketing, that's the future of advertising. It has been, I'd say, even for the past 15 years, and it's not going to slow down. And so my advice to anybody reading this book would be to pay more attention to your digital marketing strategy. Get a basic education on how digital marketing works and then just make sure you team up with the right partner to steer the strategy in the direction that you want to take your firm in.

Jason Hennessey is an internationally-recognized SEO expert, author, speaker, entrepreneur, and business executive. Since 2001, Jason has been reverse-engineering the Google algorithm as a self-taught student and practitioner of SEO and search marketing. As CEO of Hennessey Digital since 2015, Jason leads a team of 100+ digital marketing experts. Because of his reputation as an authority in legal SEO, he has grown a small consultancy into a $10M+ business that made the Inc. 5000 list for the second year in a row in 2020. A keynote speaker and frequent podcast and webinar guest, Jason is a columnist for the Washington Post and a regular contributor to Entrepreneur, Inc., and the National Law Review. He is also the author of, Law Firm SEO, described as the "holy grail of digital marketing for lawyers." Jason is a United States Air Force veteran and holds a Bachelor of Arts degree in Marketing from the University of Nevada, Las Vegas. A New York native, Jason launched his SEO career in Las Vegas and grew his reputation in the legal industry in Atlanta. He now lives in the Los Angeles area with his wife, Bridget, and their three children.

Chapter 21

LEADERSHIP, COMMITTEE MEMBERSHIP, COMMON BENEFIT

Sharon Boothe

Vice President of Programs at Mass Torts Made Perfect

From your point of view, and from where your business stands, tell us your experience regarding the subject matter, and the pros and cons regarding lawyer advertising prior to COVID.

My expertise is in helping lawyers network themselves at Mass Torts Made Perfect in Las Vegas. The big reason why lawyers from all over the country go to Vegas twice a year is because they're promoting themselves and their firms to each other to work together on cases in order to get cases referred to you, co-counsel and the local counsel for somebody. So the attorney advertising that I have experienced with this is the lawyers wanting to meet each other in order to develop their reputations in the mass tort bars so that they can work together with firms across the country.

Pre COVID, obviously, the conference was a huge part of, I think, every firm that comes to Mass Torts Made Perfect. Many of them attend both times; they come in both the fall and the spring. Prior to COVID, I think they were very used to the routine of going to Vegas twice a year, finding out what big projects were going on, who was doing what, who was expanding, and networking. It's like shooting fish in a barrel when you're in Las Vegas because it's a group, everybody's together and basically, anybody in the mass tort world that you want to meet is going to be there. If they're not there, somebody from their firm is there. So I think lawyers have really gotten used to that, the ability to go twice a year and accomplish a lot in the three days they're there–meet new people, reestablish other older relationships and have meetings. There's a ton of organizational and committee meetings and different litigation projects that go on in Vegas adjacent to the conference. I think attorneys were really used to all of the built-in ease of networking with each other that Vegas provided.

That all changed on March 16th when a national emergency was declared and nobody left their homes again. So I think that what we've been trying to do since COVID is we've pivoted to an online platform. We've been bringing lawyers together every month on webinars to talk about what's going on in mass tort litigation. We talk about not just the mass tort projects, but the marketing aspects of how do you market your firm during COVID? How do you stay on top of technology during COVID? How do you deal with not being able to get your case to trial, you know, everything? So we've gone to an online format, which has been hugely attended. And then we did our first virtual Vegas seminar last October which had a platform. Lawyers could go on the platform and do two things, they could go to the sessions and get the content on what was going on in the mass tort projects that they're interested in or involved in. Then there were all kinds of business topics like how to grow your firm during COVID, how to deal with Zoom depositions, all those kinds of things. There were networking components of the virtual event, but most people still aren't good at going to a virtual conference and figuring out how to network the way they're used to walking into a ballroom in Las

Vegas where they know exactly what to do. So we've had a really hard time teaching the lawyers, the attendees, how to make these virtual events beneficial to them and to their firms. Because we thought COVID was going to be three months, six months, nine months, but at the end of the day, it's going to end up taking close to two years out of people's ability to travel the way they're used to. That's a big change for people who were used to doing a lot of their business development face-to-face. So what we found was that we really need to continue to work with these lawyers to teach them how to accomplish some of this. They need to keep their firms going and growing and relevant and not fall by the wayside. We need to really work with them to teach them how to use these virtual formats.

Did you see a lot more attendees because it's virtual now? Or did you see a lot more when it was in person?

No, our conference was much bigger in person. So what we did with virtual was when we started doing webinars, we started doing them at the very end of March 2020. What we saw was a lot of people were coming to the online webinars that had never been to Vegas. They've been on our mailing list and we've been marketing to them for years, but they have never gone to Vegas because they're not going to spend that kind of money–they don't want to do that. So when we offered it for free, we started seeing all the hundreds and hundreds and hundreds of people who have been on our email list for years are now active but in an online world. The problem was with the people who are so used to going to Vegas and teaching them how to network online.

What is your view of the subject matter with regard to helping firms prior to COVID and your projections for the future?

Well, I think that some of what people have learned, as far as how to adapt during COVID specifically to advertising for cases and advertising themselves and their firms, I think, won't go away when we go back to more live events, and people are able to travel more and network the way they used to. Advertising for cases is different. During COVID, I think what some firms enjoyed was that more people were online in ways that they hadn't been before because everybody was stuck at a desk in front of a computer. I think that firms are trying to figure out in that landscape, how do they take advantage of the fact that there are a lot more eyeballs online these days than usual? When we go back to people going back to the office, traveling more, and all of that, I think lawyers who are trying to advertise for cases or find plaintiffs are going to have to figure out what's the new normal because they know what it was like before. Is it going to be some kind of hybrid? Nobody knows. I think that's the big unknown, and I think that what firms have learned during COVID is that they're a lot more adaptable to change and upheaval than they probably realized. So I think that what they'll find once COVID is gone, for the most part, it's never going to be gone, but that they're going to have to figure out what's the new normal and then adapt to that. Because I don't think anybody will just go back to the way things were two years ago. I think we've all kind of lived through this and now we're going to continue to evolve.

How are things changing? What industry changes have you seen because of COVID? And how should we pivot?

I think that as a whole the mass tort legal community, which is an industry, what they're going to do as they go forward through this is to start to find how they're going to do business. Again, I think that they are going to find that a lot of the things that they learned, the efficiencies that they learned and the things that helped them get through the crisis are going to be things that they can readapt to help them be even more efficient once this is over. So to me, it's kind of like we exercised muscles in the last year that we didn't have to exercise before. I actually think, in a lot of ways, it's just helped everybody because it's forced us all to reinvent the wheel. You know, you get into a complacency mode where everybody is just kind of used to plug and play, you just kind of do what you do. There are a lot of people out there who are very innovative and very entrepreneurial and creative and all of that, but this crisis forced everybody to do that. And so to me, the positive side effect of that is going to be that firms will be more aggressive in the future. I think that they will see that, you know, what doesn't kill you makes you stronger and that they can do business six different ways. That they can go down a different, completely different path and find new ways to do what they do and to grow. There was some of it before COVID, but I think there's a lot more of that feeling now with firms that actually did okay. I think a lot of them were very surprised at how well they did and how well their staff did. And the whole community kind of, you know, reinvented itself.

What do you see as the likely changes and trends coming down the pipeline because of everything we've reviewed so far?

I think that change is coming. I do think that to a certain extent, things will go back to the way they were. Lawyers will still want to travel to do their depositions in person. I don't think anybody feels like doing an online or a zoom deposition is as effective or would be their choice. So I think they're going to pick and choose when they use online tools like maybe we don't need to get everybody in a room every month for a status conference in Chicago, maybe stuff like that. It's not going to be, we all come back and everybody's just going to go to be on Zoom. People will have to go back and figure out, you know, what needs to be in person? What really benefits from being in person, versus what are we all now comfortable doing online.

As far as how firms advertise for plaintiffs and advertise their firms and all of that, I think that, again, a lot of that remains to be seen how people react, and what the market looks like, once everybody else sort of starts to go back to normal. I think it's going to end up being a decision where some of the stuff that we all thought you had to do in person, you don't. And then the stuff that we decide needs to be done in person we go back to and I think it'll maybe be more powerful than it was before.

What would be your overall advice to other lawyers moving forward in today's business and the economic climate?

I think that I would advise lawyers to continue to work with their partners in the legal services industry–the vendors and the companies that help law firms. These are the people who have really had to be entrepreneurial and creative during COVID. All of those businesses and companies that support law firms, case management, lead generation acquisition, digital marketing, social media marketing, financing for cases, all of those companies have had a lot of time to really look at their portfolios and how they work with firms and come up with new and different ways. I would really look at what innovations have been made by these businesses during this time and what works for your firm. I would also look at what the value is. What are the things that you want to get back to? What are the effective strategies that you've used before COVID that you should go back and start doing again? With the conference business, I really think that face-to-face business development and relationship building and networking has to come back, because relationships are so important to this group. They have to work together. You can't exist in the mass tort community as an island, you have to partner with other people, you can't do that on zoom, you just can't. You can have meetings and you can touch base and all of that, but I think everybody needs to figure out how to go back to developing those partnerships and relationships in person.

See how much has changed around the community and what businesses have done to pivot. And I think that the people who were really afraid of the change, and who don't, you know, embrace the positive things that came out of this, I think they'll miss out. I think that the firms that are able to continue to embrace the things about COVID that made us all more efficient, work better, work more intuitively, in a smart way, I think those are the people who are gonna come back really strong. I think that the personal injuries, single event, mass tort, business industry community is going to be very, very strong. There will be litigation that will come out of COVID. There will be business opportunities for people in the legal services industry in the post COVID world. So I think the people who are looking at what's the business opportunity that came out of this, I think those people are going to have success as well.

Is there anything else you would like to add to the chapter about your business or anything you'd like to mention about mass torts?

Well, I think that mass torts made perfect what we really want to take away from COVID as a business. Prior to COVID we relied 100% on in-person events where people came to Vegas twice a year. So we pivoted to online content. We now offer four to eight webinars a month on all different topics and we will never stop doing those webinars. We will continue to do that because what we've seen through COVID is, like I said at the very beginning, all those people who don't go to Vegas will connect with each other on an online program. We want to keep talking to those people. We want to keep developing relationships with that group. We also want to keep the mass tort community connected during the year when we're not in Vegas. Before COVID we would go to Vegas, it'd be this amazing business development for everybody who was there, 1800 people, and then everybody would go back to their offices and we would see each other six months later. Now, we will always have monthly webinars. We will always be keeping people connected between seminars because I think we all found out how important connection was when it got taken away from us. And I think we will now always do content and community building throughout the year and still get together twice a year in Vegas, but we will continue to connect the community during those downtimes because we've seen that that is a very powerful method and it works really well. I think it helps keep the mass tort community stronger. So that's a change we will have made that will be ongoing.

Do you think you're going to continue with the webinars after everyone's loved being in person?

Yeah, and it's funny because we used to say, back before COVID, we would say we should keep talking to our audience. Even after we all go back to Vegas, we should do a newsletter. We were always trying to come up with something, or we should do a one-day program where people can get together. And in a city, you know, not Vegas, in Los Angeles or New York or whatever. And we always kind of brush it off and then we would go back and daily life would happen, and you just kind of forget about it, and then all of a sudden, we're planning for Vegas again. I really think what we've seen is putting on these webinars is an awesome way to keep the conversation going between conferences. We got great participation and hundreds and hundreds of lawyers on every webinar. We've been able to cover topics like diversity. What does the mass tort community need to learn about how to communicate with minority plaintiffs and how to get minority law firms more involved with traditional mass tort law firms, which, by and large, are all white.

We've been able to talk about women's issues, women's career development. We've talked about time management for paralegals. How to not be drinking out of a firehose with what we've talked about. We've developed a whole paralegal series, we've never done anything for paralegals before, but the paralegals were right there with the lawyers trying to figure out how to get through this. So we developed all this paralegal content and those webinars were hugely attended.

So I think that it's been really, really interesting for us to see how much of an appetite there is for ongoing content, and I think that will stay even when people go back to traveling and everything. I think the one thing everybody's figured out is how to work anywhere. you can sign on to a webinar when you're sitting in a lobby in a building with your computer open or if you're sitting in the parking lot waiting for your kid to get done in the library or when you're using their Wi-Fi. I think that the one thing that this shows everybody is you can pretty much work anywhere all the time which is what we will take away from all this.

Getting back to Vegas, this is a very social group. And both the vendors and the legal services industry people and the lawyers, these are social creatures, If you are not, you don't go into this business. You're not attracted to this arena if you're not a social person. And so it's funny because I think that a lot of us have learned how to do what we do just via Zoom. This is a group that needs to connect. They need to be together and a lot can happen when you're living on the ground in Vegas. So many meetings happen. So many off the cuff, "Oh, hey, you don't know this guy." Or "Oh, come over here. Let's sit down. Let's go get a coffee," and "You two should work together." I mean, so much of that goes on that when people can get back to that face-to-face they will resume doing that because you can't recreate that online. You have to set up the meeting and schedule it and invite the people and all that. When you're in Vegas, you're just walking down the hallways and everybody's there. Everybody who's anybody is there. And it's just so easy to get a lot done and you can't replace that. So I feel like my job security is good because I think live events will come back.

Sharon Boothe is Vice President of Programs at Mass Torts Made Perfect and oversees the entire MTMP portfolio of programs. This includes the MTMP live seminars in Las Vegas twice a year, the MTMP Connect monthly webinars, and the MTMP Connect Paralegal College monthly webinars. She also oversees the fundraising arm of MTMP and has organized auctions to support the American Association for Justice and the Sheller Center for Social Justice at Temple Law School in Philadelphia. Sharon also serves as the Executive Director of the Trial Lawyer Hall of Fame at Temple Law School, which houses portraits and interactive content of the lives of Hall of Fame inductees. Additionally, Sharon is Director of Operations for TrialSchool.Org, an online skills and training membership-based organization for personal injury and mass tort plaintiff lawyers. Prior to joining MTMP in 2011, Sharon was President of HB Litigation Conferences and started her career in 1991, launching the Mealey's Conference division of Mealey Publications.

Chapter 22

MASS TORT NEWS

Mark A. York

Editor - Mass Tort News

Tell me your experience regarding the subject matter and the pros and cons regarding lawyer advertising prior to COVID and now.

Prior to COVID, lawyer advertising was very widespread. And there were numerous torts that people were involved in and money was pouring into dockets. I mean, there was enormous amounts of money being spent. It was generally whatever the flavor of the day was, whether it was an MDL or a state court consolidation. And there were at any one time 12 or 15 of the various major torts going on that people were just pouring money into because it was just business as usual–the mass tort machine was moving forward.

Since COVID has started, things have changed quite a bit. Not generally so much, because the courts have stopped moving things forward. But everything slowed down for about six months because there was a readjustment both at law firms and vendors, etc. People were working remotely. They had to wrap their arms around how to do that in certain torts, some of the activity that was pending, and people started being more selective about what they were going into as far as certain activities. Many of the mid-level mass tort firms or the new entry firms were holding back because they did not know what the end result of COVID-19 was going to be as far as their law firm practice. So some people were holding on to what would have been marketing money or other expenditures based on a wait-and-see attitude. And actually, the wait-and-see attitude still exists right now. Because no one is sure when things are going to get back to somewhat normal. I would say that there are the top 20% of the firms that will keep on spending extravagantly large amounts of money in marketing and getting the cases and moving things forward. Then there's that mid-level group that is still somewhat cautious about expenditures, whether it's getting into new torts or other things. It's a wait-and-see attitude that seems to be still in place to a certain degree. People are being conservative, a little bit more conservative than they were.

What's your view of the subject matter with regard to helping law firms prior to COVID and your projections for the future?

Prior to COVID, I can tell you that law firms were very aggressive in what they were doing looking at new torts, engaging in new torts, consulting, business interacting, whether it was on participation with other firms outside, third party consulting, things like that, as well as just expanding ongoing torts. Firms were very, very aggressive Prior to COVID. Post COVID, I can tell you from my own firsthand experience, a fairly good number of firms started severing consulting relationships, tightening up their outside vendor relationships. Where they may have had five marketing relationships with various marketing companies, they dialed that down to two. They really became much more conservative in the number of parties that they were dealing with, and their expenditures to outside third parties. Post COVID, I do know for a fact that many of the law firms became much more restrictive in their interaction with outside parties, they kind of circled their wagons and they maintained a determined, predetermined level that they wanted to keep. And they kind of proceeded down that road. Things are opening up a little bit more now and law firms are becoming more receptive to interacting generally, and more social about things. Even in media participation, it got to a point where people working from home and remotely, seemed to be causing a lack of communication. Whereas before where people were going into an office, you did whatever the work functions were; and, that meant talking, interacting on media, and communication on other things. Once COVID hit, communications just slowed down extensively.

It's opening up now. In the last 60 days, people have gotten a little bit more casual. The National Trial Lawyers Summit May 4th-7th in Miami should be the first live event that's going forward. The Lanier Trial Academy in Houston is coming in June. That's live. So you know, those things are opening back up. But then again, the MTMP (Mass Torts Made Perfect) seminar, I think it's in April, is a webcast version. So there's contrasting views on certain things. I don't know, it could be that May 1st might be the day that it's announced that COVID is cured.

What industry changes have you seen because of COVID and how should we pivot?

Well, first, the most direct thing I've seen is the perception that a law practice is a law office, a brick and mortar office. That's changed extensively, as well as the labor requirement and the management style. The firms that were able to adapt were the ones that had good employee hiring practices previously, and good stable managers and employees. So whenever everyone started working remotely the bosses in the big, corner offices were like, "Oh, my God, no works gonna get done." But after a couple of months it just kind of evolved and those same people were like, "Whoa, we are still moving forward and the doors didn't fall off" or anything like that. And that showed that they were adults about it. I can tell you from talking to many, many lawyers, professionals, not just in the legal world, that people for the first 60 days when told they would be working from home were saying, "Oh, sweet, I'm working from home, I can do whatever I want all day." That lasted about 45 to 60 days. And then they got into the rut of, "My God, I'm working at home." They had no change, especially those who have children. Being full-time at home made them realize that the time away actually allowed them to think outside the box a little bit more professionally. People started adapting where they had no-go zones in their house, where they created their offices. Some people turned their garages into offices, I do know that. So everyone adapted very, very differently. Now some offices are getting back to having people come into the office as soon as possible to kind of restore what was going on pre-COVID. But there are other firms that are saying we may never return to the punching-a-clock type thing because everything seems to be moving forward. There are numerous new vendors and a law firm practice, management programs, zoom video, go to meetings, go to webinars, those are all doing phenomenally well, business-wise, because everyone's getting comfortable with that. I do think it takes away the personal interaction between vendors and law firms, that personal interaction and discussions, like happens at events and shows, 75% of that is gone. And so that has a significant impact on one-to-one interaction, which helps a lot in vendor law firm relationships. I think people have learned to adapt and move things forward, and it's going to be a blend, regardless. If three months from now COVID is done they're gonna say it's working the way we have it. Everything is functioning the way we want so they may reconsider re-upping that 20,000 square foot lease. They may now realize they can cut their lease requirements in half, hard financial costs that people are going to be analyzing. I'm sure that just staffing requirements have become a little bit leaner, because you don't have an office to support, you just have a network of people loosely affiliated working from home generally. So that's just kind of more of the practice support policy side.

I actually talked to someone who by bringing in those webinars has expanded their reach and they said they will continue their online presence even after we are able to resume meeting in person.

I have mass tort news legalcasts, which are gaining in popularity. But then again, there's oversaturation because everybody is doing webinars about this. Pretty soon, it's gonna be like cable TV, if you look after two o'clock in the morning, if you're going down the guide, there are 60 infomercials there, and there's like ten things on television. So it's kind of like that, where people are just inundated with every kind of webinar all the time. So keeping a unique way of doing the webinars and the subject matter is going to have people coming out with new ideas which are always going to attract more attention. But even that will wear off because it's just becoming much less expensive to put on webinars than it is to put on live events and shows. So people figured that out pretty quickly.

What do you see as likely changes and trends coming down the pipe because of everything we've talked about so far?

One of the things is that social media has become saturated, because that was the easiest, fastest way to get into some of the trends in the marketing aspect. And there's getting to be a lot of new players that are well funded, and they have the ability to offer a very good product. There's always going to be the two or three major players out there, I'm not going to say any names, but they're always going to be there. There will also be the new and emerging companies because people recognize that there's a lot of revenue being generated in mass torts in the advertising side for various reasons, and they're gonna want to capitalize on that. Anytime there is an influx of money into a certain area, it's much easier to have someone just run a social media campaign than it is to go through the whole process of all the other ways marketing used to be done. There are so many other ways now. It's just a little bit different because people are paying much more attention and they have people that have developed, by necessity, as part of the COVID situation. Sitting at home for six or seven hours, you start paying attention to things that you might have casually overlooked because pre-COVID the mass tort assembly line was running smoothly. Suddenly things were interrupted at various phases and stages for each firm. Those relationships with some vendors went away, some law firms kind of ran into issues. People started really analyzing and reviewing the who, what, where, and how the trends are going to be. I think everything is going to be operated on a much leaner scale. With regard to production, people want analytics and numbers and data and that's how some of the decisions are going to be made. Where before at the events you had personal relationships that were long term and ongoing because every time you went to some of the major events, you saw person x, or attorney x, and you rekindle that relationship, whether it was drinks, dinner, just talking and catching up and remembering the good times. That's an opportunity that's not been there for over a year now. I think it's coming up, but it'll be a year. So that personal interaction is not there. So it's either a Zoom call, or a phone call or a text or an email. And that just doesn't replace personal interaction. So the trends I think are going to be a little bit more written and more kind of a remote relationship, at least for the short term until things get back to normal and people get back to attending events again and rekindle their long-term relationships.

What would be your overall advice to other lawyers moving forward in today's business and economic climate?

Think outside the box 100%. In media and then in mass tort consulting to a degree, I would say, always look for alternatives. Keep your relationships and who you're dealing with and talking to, whether it's on a personal or professional vendor level, look at the other options. Always have a backup plan. Especially in light of COVID, have a backup plan and then have a backup plan for that backup plan. That means that you're talking to two or three vendors, and you have a preferred person, there's nothing wrong with having a backup just in case something goes awry. Because as you know, some of the entities that have been around could experience business interruptions. In other words, some of these companies you've been dealing with for X amount of time are no longer there. So, it's always good to have something as a backup plan, a transition plan to go from one thing to another. I think working remotely and Zoom is here to stay. Zoom, GoToMeeting, and all those remote meeting systems are here to stay no matter what because of the convenience. Start looking at the money that's saved in all these other areas, you can apply them into your mass tort dockets. There are some firms that used to have 20 lawyers traveling all the time. Now, they're just doing Zoom and other E-discussions, and that makes a huge difference financially. So I would say keep communicating, attending, going to the webinars and just getting your reach out there. Be prepared for changes in the new versus the old school way. COVID drastically changed the whole perception of business, healthcare, society, travel, recreation, vacation, it just changed everything around the world.

Is there anything else you want to include? You mentioned your collaboration with Bloomberg?

For the media outreach side, framing public opinion, strategic public relations, whether it is your firm's message about a docket or a specific case, can never be underestimated. What takes place today that someone just might read innocuously might have an effect somewhere down the road. Keep in mind that your target audience for a lot of what you're doing for public opinion, is not other lawyers. Don't limit yourself to trying to do lawyer to lawyer interaction in your media and outreach to the general public or mass media and think just the regular mainstream media. Not the fake news, of course, because there's a lot of that, but, there are ways to get your messaging out. One is Mass Tort News. You can contribute, co-author anything there. That's an example of actual news where media releases go out that aren't slanted towards a specific docket for referral purposes or something like that, which a lot of the media is in the legal world because it's an industry-driven subject.

Mark A. York is known for research and writing in emerging complex litigation including the opioid crisis and other Mass Torts as well as consulting with professional service firms. His career includes working at major law firms and corporate legal departments throughout the United States primarily in Intellectual Property/Complex Commercial Litigation, Corporate Regulatory Compliance, and Corporate Due Diligence review. These firms include Schiff Hardin, LLP; Locke, Lord, Edwards LLP and Arnold, White & Durkee, as well as Westinghouse Nuclear Design Systems; Newell-Rubbermaid and Northrop-Grumman Corp. where he was active in white collar and intellectual property investigations and white-collar compliance guidance. Mark began his business career with Encyclopaedia Britannica, N.A. as a Federal Regulatory Compliance Director, while monitoring, enforcing and directing worldwide compliance issues. These professional law firm relationships continue to this day in select projects.

Chapter 23

OPERATING A MASS TORT LAW FIRM DURING COVID

Joseph Fantini

Managing Attorney of Rosen Injury Lawyers' Mass Tort Department

Tell us your experience regarding the subject matter and the pros and cons regarding lawyer advertising prior to COVID and now

With regard to mass torts, a lot of our clients are found online. So during the COVID pandemic, with more people being home, and being online, I found that it was easier to get in touch with the clients. We still use a bunch of different platforms, but a very effective medium to reach the clients was digital marketing and also some of the TV advertisements. I would say that there was a decrease overall in some of the billboard advertisements and the responses that we would see to that because less people would be out driving around and seeing those advertisements. I have seen that clients have definitely been a lot more responsive during this pandemic and our response rate to our advertisements and then also our response rates to getting in touch with the clients after they submitted an inquiry has increased. But some of the cons, like I said, some of the other forms of marketing that we've traditionally used have not been as successful.

What is your view of the subject matter with regard to helping law firms prior to COVID and what are your projections for the future?

I think we could definitely learn a lot from what occurred over the past year. And I think with regard to mass tort marketing, it's going where the clients are. So what other platform they're using at that time. You have to be able to adapt and get in front of the clients because unlike car accidents, or slip and falls, they may not be aware of these products and the harms that they cause. Being able to get in front of the clients on a lot of different platforms is really important. So instead of investing in billboards, or maybe some of the more traditional print media, you need to have a lot of different avenues and resources to reach out to the clients. I think that's something that people and law firms should definitely become more familiar with. It's something that's going to be around for a long time. So the clients now are much more apt at getting information from a bunch of different sources, so you'll be dealing with a more educated client. That's going to help everybody, the law firm, and also the clients moving forward here.

What industry changes have you seen because of COVID? And how should we pivot?

I think overall, in mass tort cases similar to a lot of other personal injury cases, it really slowed down the opportunity to get our clients in front of a jury, which is ultimately our goal. So what it showed us is that you really need to be able to be flexible and adapt to the circumstances, but always have your cases as ready as possible to move forward, whether it's towards settlement or mediation, or trial, but being flexible and being creative with ways to get the cases resolved. That's something that was a challenge at the beginning of COVID. But myself and other members of the bar have really embraced the technology. I think that's helped us move the cases forward. And if there's any sort of pandemic or other circumstances in the future, we can use the tools that we developed during this time to help continue to move the cases forward, and also employ those same tactics when we're not dealing with a crisis like this.

What do you see as likely changes and trends coming down the pipe because of everything we've talked about so far?

Going forward, I really expect to continue to see a more educated client out there because there's a lot of information that's available to them. I expect them to reach out to a number of different law firms and be well versed in the law firms background and their past results and what to expect going forward. The clients also want us to cater to them and go to the different platforms that they're on. I think whatever the next platform is, lawyers are going to have to be flexible and go there. You know, ten years ago, people weren't doing any marketing on Facebook. And now a big number of spends are focused on Facebook. Twenty years ago, people were focusing more on television, billboards and print media, and they're now getting away from that. So being able to adapt and get in front of the clients with valuable information, instead of just an advertisement, is what they want to see. It's something that we're going to continue to do at Rosen Injury Lawyers and I expect my colleagues to do as well.

What would be your overall advice to other lawyers moving forward in today's business and economic climate?

I would just advise my colleagues here to have a diverse portfolio. So we've seen some other industries have some challenges, whether it was during the pandemic, the foreclosure law firms, or the traditional personal injury law firms, where there weren't as many accidents or slip and falls so having a diverse portfolio will help you. Especially in mass tort, I think that it would be helpful to have a bunch of different cases that you're working on at the same time, a bunch of different torts, so that the process is never fully brought to a halt. Then adapting and using technology as a tool, instead of being hesitant and resistant to change. That's going to be your best avenue going forward with a diverse practice area, and a diverse number of cases and torts that you're working on.

I think this pandemic taught us to always really expect the unexpected, and you really have to be as flexible as possible, and adapt to whatever comes about whether it was having everybody work remotely, whether it was the courts being closed, or the issues with the mail, you just have to be able to problem-solve. And I think that's what trial attorneys are good at doing. So in these uncertain times, coming up with solutions to always move the client's case forward and operate in their best interest. That's something that we've learned here at Rosen Injury Lawyers and will continue as we move forward.

Joseph Fantini serves as the managing attorney of Rosen Injury Lawyers' Mass Tort Department. His practice focuses on representing victims injured by dangerous pharmaceutical drugs, defective medical devices and unsafe consumer products. Joe's background and understanding of complex medical, scientific and legal issues has positioned him to be a leader in national Mass Tort Litigations. Joe obtained his law degree from the esteemed Widener University School of Law in 2009. While in law school, Joe was the recipient of the Certificate of Achievement in Food and Drug Law, which is awarded to the top student in each section.

It was during this time that Joe was first exposed to the intricacies of FDA regulations and oversight. After learning of the devastating injuries suffered by consumers of defective products that were unsafe and inadequately tested, Joe knew he wanted to lend his voice to those who were unable to fight these large corporations who placed profits over patient's safety on their own. Joe began his career as a lawyer at an international insurance defense firm, where he represented clients in personal injury and product liability matters. After just a few years, Joe moved to a nationally recognized plaintiff's law firm to represent plaintiffs' mass torts and class actions. In 2018, Joe joined Rosen Injury Lawyers to manage the Mass Tort Department and oversee all product liability cases. As a result of his achievements, Joe has been included in Pennsylvania Super Lawyers publication as a Rising Star, a distinction given to only 2.5% of attorneys in each state who are forty years old or younger or have been practicing for ten years or less, continuously since 2013. Joe has also been recognized as The National Trial Lawyers: Top 40 Under 40 and is a member of The National Trial Lawyers: Top 25 Mass Tort Trial Lawyers Association. Additionally, Joe is a member of the Pennsylvania Association for Justice, Philadelphia Bar Association, and the Philadelphia Trial Lawyers Association, where he serves as a member of the Young Lawyers executive committee.

THANK YOU FOR
READING THIS BOOK

DOWNLOAD YOUR FREE GIFTS

Just to say thanks for buying and reading my book, I would like
to give you a few free bonus gifts, no strings attached.

To Download Now, Visit:
www.MasstortsAtoZbook.com/Freegifts

I appreciate your interest in my book, and I value your feedback as it helps me
improve future versions of this book. I would appreciate it if you could leave your
invaluable review on Amazon.com with your feedback. Thank you!

Made in the USA
Las Vegas, NV
19 October 2022

57730027R10072